Penelope Down East

The Marshall 22 Catboat

Length overall: 22' 2"
Length at the waterline: 21' 4"
Beam: 10' 4"
Draft: 2' 0" (board up)
        5' 2" (board down)
Sail Area: 388 square feet
Displacement: 5660 pounds
Ballast: 850 pounds

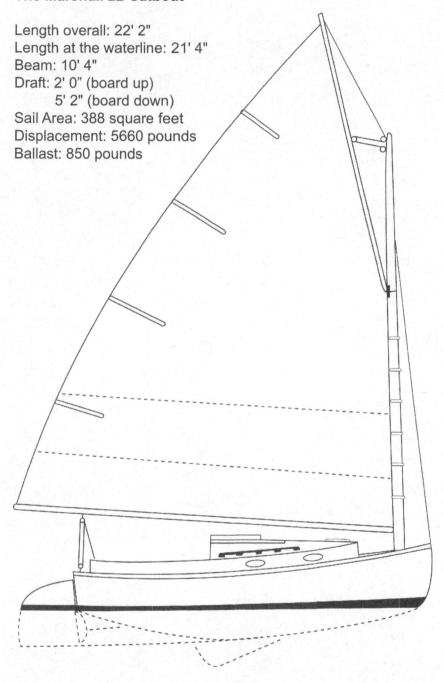

Penelope
Down
East

Cruising Adventures
in an Engineless Catboat
Along the World's
Most Beautiful Coast

W. R. CHENEY

BREAKAWAY BOOKS

HALCOTTSVILLE, NEW YORK

2015

Penelope Down East:
    Cruising Adventures in an Engineless Catboat Along the World's Most Beautiful Coast

Copyright © 2015 by W. R. Cheney
ISBN: 978-1-62124-018-1
Library of Congress Control Number: 2015945488

Published by Breakaway Books
P.O. Box 24
Halcottsville, NY 12438
www.breakawaybooks.com

Portions of some of these stories have appeared in *Points East, Messing About in Boats, Maine Boats, Homes, and Harbors,* and the bulletin of the Catboat Association.

FIRST PRINTING

For Kendra,

my delightful companion on the biggest adventure of all.

They are given motors,
and that damns them, as boats, for all time.

—Conor O'Brien

Contents

Foreword

Bill Cheney is a fine sailor, storyteller, and wordsmith. Put together, it's no surprise that he has given us a fine collection of sailing stories.

If you have heard much about cruising the fabled coast of Maine and, as yet, have never done so, here is the vicarious experience you have been waiting for.

If you *have* cruised this iconic, watery world, as I have, and want a companion to share many of your favorite bays, islands, harbors . . . and to introduce you to new experiences and places . . . here you will find your soul mate and guide.

Sometimes you *can* judge a book by the cover. The special qualities that distinguish this tidy little volume and its author are all suggested in the subtitle:

"Cruising"

Many set out for a day sail along Maine's coast. We pick a day with obliging winds, weather, and tides. And we're back home for a shower and supper.

Cruising is another matter. You may think you know the conditions coming in a day or two. After that you have no choice but to deal with whatever may come. And come it will: rains, winds, fogs, seas . . . and mosquitoes.

"World's Most Beautiful Coast"

I've cruised in the San Juan Islands, the Bahamas, Florida, the Virgin Islands, the Greek Isles, and San Francisco Bay. None of these sites is as overwhelmingly beautiful, varied, and enchanting as the Maine coast. And none is as daunting and dangerous. The dense fogs, the lurking ledges, the rip currents, the sudden squalls, and the lobster pot buoys are legendary.

The gods may protect beginning sailors and fools . . . sometimes both. But not along the coast of Maine.

We will learn in what follows that cruising Maine offers much for the heart . . . but not for the faint of heart.

"Catboat"

As one who sails a catboat in the benign Florida Everglades waters I can attest to how much fun awaits at the helm of this lively little craft and how manageable is the single sheet and sail.

But as one who sails a full-keeled sloop on the Maine coast, I can attest to how especially unforgiving conditions there can be for a shallow-draft, centerboarded vessel with a huge mainsail. These little craft can have trouble in heavy seas. They may take a knockdown . . . and they can capsize.

As Bill Cheney demonstrates, it takes considerable courage and skill to sail and cruise a catboat in these inhospitable waters. Hubris won't do it.

"Engineless"

On boats equipped with power, the captain can assure those

ashore, those on board, and himself that he knows where he is going and about when he will get there. Not so aboard the boat without engine. Cheney's mantra can sometimes be most troubling and insufficient to others. "It will depend on the way the wind blows."

Added to the monumental challenges of cruising the bony coast of Maine in a shallow-draft catboat, doing so without an engine is all the more remarkable.

Our captain is a purist. His distrust and distaste for the infernal combustion engine are matched by only the fascinating repertoire of means he has developed for getting along without one.

Herein lies one of the most valuable contributions of this little book to each of us who has been—or will be—inevitably faced with the panic that comes when "it" won't start or run. Anchor? Drift? Wait? Row? Or even accept a tow? Panic for us; only an intriguing puzzle to be solved for him.

I would add only one other quality so significant in this volume that is not found in the title:

Single-Handed

There are two actors in this collection of stories: the author and *Penelope*, his vessel.

Bill Cheney is not a youngster, nor is his nearly half-century-old catboat. Together these senior citizens form a trusting, affectionate bond . . . as in "We entered the cove carefully."

But *Penelope* is usually his *only* companion on these adventures. This means but one pair of hands must haul and coil anchor; raise, lower, reef, and furl the massive sail; adjust sail trim; plot and hold a course; spot navigation aids; free that pot buoy from the rudder . . . and retrieve and open a can of beer. Frequently all at once. Try it sometime!

So this, dear reader, is the collection of remarkable qualities that will make reading *Penelope Down East* an engaging, noteworthy pleasure. Preferably in your rocking chair in front of the winter fire or in your cockpit or bunk after an exhausting day at sea.

In addition, in these pages you will discover a few other gifts. As any cruiser knows, sailing is punctuated by unexpected, charming, memorable, sometimes interminable non-nautical moments. Like encountering a praying mantis, cooking a gourmet dinner over a can of Sterno, or talking with a kindred spirit in harbor. Stir into the pot elements of seamanship such as tending the mooring, anchoring, and bottom painting, and you end up with a sailing handbook.

But for me, the central question asked—and fully answered—here is: So how *does* one sail and cruise the Maine coast, alone, aboard an engineless catboat . . . and live to tell and write about it? Very prudently, serenely . . . and joyfully.

Come aboard with skipper Bill Cheney and savor the passages that follow!

—**Roland Sawyer Barth**, author of *Tales of the Intracoastal Waterway: An Account of a Passage from the Florida Keys to Cape Cod in a Seventeen Foot Catboat,* Head Tide, Maine, 2015

Introduction

Sometime around my eighth birthday my uncle Lee started letting me use his clamming skiff. He kept her tied up down in a narrow creek called "the dreen" that ran up into a marsh from Shinnecock Bay on the South Shore of Long Island, New York.

I would walk a mile or so through piney woods and scrub oak, down a long two-track sandy dirt road, past the "mud house," an odd igloo-shaped, adobe-walled, sea-shell-studded summer dwelling built by an eccentric cousin, to the bay. A path along shore led to the dreen, and to Uncle Lee's skiff, the *Eel*, moored to a piling and waiting for me. *Eel* seemed an odd name for her because she was, in fact, short and fat.

Heavy, flat-bottomed, and painted battleship gray, *Eel* was equipped with a dangerous-looking (many exposed moving parts) outboard that had been marketed by Sears, Roebuck & Company under the trade name of Water Witch.

My ticket as an eight-year-old neophyte mariner did not include permission to operate "the Water Bitch"—as she had been aptly renamed by the many relatives who had so frequently tried, but failed, to start and run her. The Bitch specialized in merrily powering parties across the bay to a buoy near the Ponquogue Bridge where the flounder fishing was good and then rejecting all efforts to restart her, leaving the party with a very log, weary row home, usually against wind and tide.

My ticket was for rowing only, and it was just as well. Not only was I in for healthy exercise, but along the way I developed a distrust of and distaste for engines on boats that has led in the end to my happy embrace of engineless cruising.

I would untie *Eel* and row out of the dreen into Shinnecock Bay where I hung a left, heading east.

Going east, I could row along shore past my aunt Alice's Pine Grove House and on past bayman and duck hunting guide Uncle Fred's imposing shoreside domain. Frequently octogenarian Uncle Fred could be seen tending the extensive clam beds he maintained off his house. In those days a clammer with waterfront property (now, alas, an oxymoron in today's era of astronomical shorefront property tax) would harvest clams off the dunes on the east side of the bay and replant them off his house on the west side, thus enabling him to wait for favorable market prices.

Some of the houses along the shore had long docks going out into the bay, and off those docks were moored graceful open cat-boats, most of them built by my grandmother's first cousin Uncle Frank Carter at his shop in East Quogue.

There were Gil Smith boats from down Patchogue way, too, but although the Smith boats tended to be fancier and boasted more exotic woods—cherry and pear and such—Uncle Frank's boats were their equal on the water.

These catboats, both Uncle Frank's and Gil Smith's, were the aristocrats of the bay, and I wanted one from a very early age.

My longshore trips took me as far as the Caffrey House, a rambling boardinghouse run for summer guests from New York City by Fred's sister, my great-grandmother Emmaline (née Squires), and her spinster daughter, my aunt Minerva.

If I was lucky there would be leftover apple fritters or pie at the Caffrey House, and thus fortified I would head back for the dreen, always admiring the catboats along the way.

There was always a galvanized bucket in Uncle Lee's skiff, and I have always liked them. Now that I have catboats of my own, the venerable and somehow majestic *Penelope* for summers in Maine and the sprightly Marshall Sanderling *Shorebird* for winters in the Low Country of South Carolina, I make sure to have galvanized buckets aboard. I've got three in *Penelope*, and two in the smaller *Shorebird*.

A friend of mine, whom I recently took for a sail in *Penelope*, remarked on the three buckets and asked what they were for. "That one holds sail ties and miscellaneous stuff," I said. "That one is the pee bucket, and that one is just because I like galvanized buckets."

I love the sounds they make banging around in the cockpit as we prepare for a day on the water. They remind me of the bucket in the *Eel* and it takes me right back.

I did own a cat-rigged sailing dinghy in my teens, and I enjoyed many an adventure with her, but I had to wait long years before I had a true cruising catboat of my own. A number of years as a photojournalist in Europe and a war in Vietnam came first. Then work in New York City and, later, Vermont got in the way. Even during those years I managed to own a couple of cruising sloops and do some fairly serious voyaging, but it wasn't until much later in life that I had *Penelope*, a true cruising catboat, and was at last able to fulfill the dreams engendered by my longshore cruises in Uncle Lee's clamming skiff.

It would not be on Shinnecock Bay, but on the wider and breathtakingly beautiful expanses of the Maine coast, and it was worth the wait.

The reader may notice that while there are frequent mentions of places like McGlathery Island, Orcutt Harbor, and Castine in the narratives that follow, there is little or nothing about Rockland, Camden, Belfast, Searsport, or Winter Harbor. I've sailed *Penelope* to all these places and more, but I've limited my remarks to places where I've had unusually interesting experiences, pleasant or otherwise.

Rockland, for example, is great for art galleries and gourmet restaurants, and Camden is good for its bookstores and a wonderful grocery close by the town dock. But this is not a book about shopping trips.

Belfast offers poor shelter in weather from several directions, and anchoring is not allowed in the inner harbor (a symptom of a creeping disease that is coming slowly up the coast from more congested areas to the west and south). There is also at least one seafood restaurant that cuts you off after a single glass of Chardonnay. My lone visit to that town was not a lot of fun, but no doubt I am being unfair to a place that, I'm told, has a lot going for it.

Winter Harbor, at the other end of our cruising grounds, has a diner that serves up great haddock sandwiches, but otherwise offers mostly a lot of very deep water to anchor in, and not much else.

The reader may also note that my descriptions of waterborne culinary strategies vary considerably from chapter to chapter. This is because the various chapters were written over a number of years, and my approach to cooking afloat has been subject to constant evolution.

I always ate well, however, and some of my best gustatory experiences date back to a time when my approach was at its simplest and most primitive. The best meal I ever had on a boat took place many years ago in Newport, Rhode Island. It was fresh swordfish cooked over a can of Sterno. As I think back on it now, I believe that improbably exquisite repast ranks among the very best I ever enjoyed anywhere.

I hope my time on the water has brought with it some valuable lessons. Some of these I propose to share with the reader, along with many of the experiences I have enjoyed here and there along this most beautiful of coasts, be they happy or otherwise.

I feel privileged to say that happy has been the dominant theme, far outweighing anything else, and that, in my advancing years, I would give anything to be able to start all over again, right from the beginning.

A Word on Sailing in Maine Waters

The predominating features of Maine waters are hard rock shores and innumerable islands. The passages between the rocky shores of those islands tend to be deep, and the shores themselves are generally steep-to, dropping off dramatically. When there are hazards close to shore, the water is clear, and objects below the surface are usually visible at some depth.

I find these conditions considerably less treacherous than in other cruising areas where sandy or muddy shoals reach out far from shore and hazards are less obviously apparent. This is particularly true in the many places where the water lacks Maine's lucid transparency.

On the rare occasions when I venture offshore from inlets along the barrier islands of South Carolina and Georgia, I shudder with terror at the thought of invisible sandbars seven or eight miles from land. I just don't like it out there.

Not so in Maine with its formidable but straightforward hazards. I have a reasonable expectation that I will never, as I once did when passing over an invisible shoal in Vineyard Sound, look down between large, cresting rollers and see bare white sand. The gods were with us that day, and we never touched, but I say give me deep water and honest rocks any day. Your chances of seeing them or hearing them are much better.

Fog is what most people "from away" think of when they think of danger along the Maine coast, and certainly it can be a problem. But you get used to it. I would even say that you can come to like it. Back in the days before global positioning devices made everything so much easier, it used to be fun to go out and navigate by sound, smell, and feel. When you learned that you could locate islands by smell, or the feel of warmer air coming off them, or the sound of waves breaking on shore, you began to feel like a real sailor.

Nowadays nothing is invisible, no matter how thick the fog. The old skills die as we all rely on the little electronic magic boxes to show the way. My only advice here is to carry at least two of these devices because, now that we depend on them, it is an awful feeling when that screen goes dead. There is no going back.

All boats in Maine waters should carry a serious radar reflector, too, and a powerful horn. The lobstermen don't stop working when the fog rolls in. They continue at their usual rather frenetic pace, and they need a way to know where you are.

Needless to say the major shipping lanes are no place for a small boat to be in fog, but this is not really much of a problem except around Portland or, occasionally, when a tanker is making its way up Penobscot Bay, bound for Searsport. There is, additionally, a growing presence of large cruise ships, from the *QE II* on down, in places along the coast that are not easy to predict. If this is a worry, it might be best to restrict one's foggy-day excursions to relatively shallow areas where the damn things can't go.

Finally there is that mixed blessing: the ubiquitous lobster buoy. In summer they blossom around every harbor and shore. You just can't get away from them unless you go way offshore. The bad thing about them is that if you motor over one, or in some cases even sail over it, it will catch your prop or rudder. This is unfortunate for you who will lose time and suffer aggravation, and for the lobsterman who may lose his expensive and hard-earned gear. Try to be gentle in such circumstances. Cut yourself free if you have to, but try to hold on to both ends and tie them back together before you go.

The good thing about lobster buoys is that their presence almost always indicates a depth of water that is navigable for most boats. A single buoy may have drifted into shoal water, but a whole raft of them can be counted on without question.

The presence of the lobster buoy, of course, indicates the existence of the lobsterman, and, believe it, he is your friend. He may break some of your china as his massive wake provides an unwelcome wakeup call in your quiet early-morning anchorage while he roars off to work, and he may even enjoy doing it, but if you ever really need him, he will be there to help. And most competent and generous help it will be.

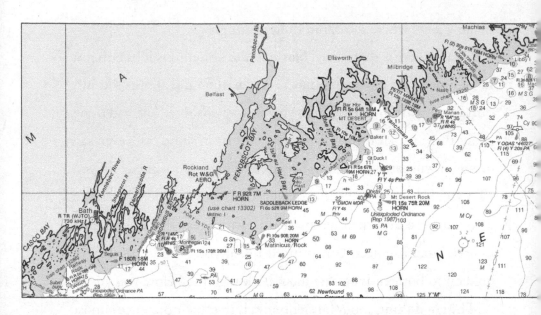

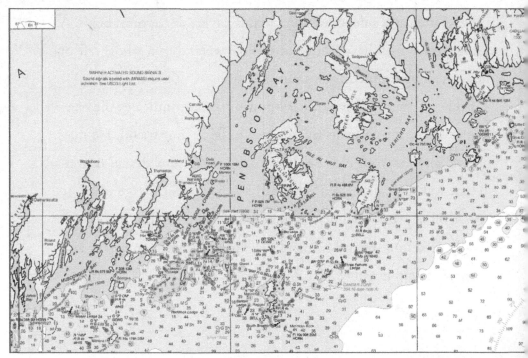

1. The Case Against Old Thumper

A long and eventful day on the water winds up with a tricky beat up a narrow channel into a perfect, almost landlocked gunkhole. All day we have reached and run among the breathtakingly beautiful islands of the mid-Maine coast and now, to top it off, there is this difficult beat into harbor.

We charge toward shore, cutting it close, until sinister rocks show green and menacing in the water just ahead, then luff, tack over, and head for the other side. We like to push the limits. We feel confident in our ability to read shore and water, and we know what our boat will do. This testing dance is the very best part of an entire day of good moments in our engineless boat.

In harbor now, anchored and squared away, I watch a handsome sloop, sails all neatly furled, motor in through the same stretch. No testing dance for him. Earlier in the day, I had seen this same boat motoring downwind in the Eggemoggin Reach. I wondered then as I often do, what is the point of having a sailboat if you don't sail it?

I wonder about that, and I also reflect that while those who rely overmuch on the starter button may benefit from a measure of convenience, they are missing out on a very large portion of the joys and challenges that come with pure sailing.

~

My own conversion to the simpler and more self-sufficient ways of an earlier time began way back with my uncle Lee's clamming skiff, the *Eel*, when I didn't have any choice. But for years as owner of a series of cruising boats, I still subscribed to the common notion that an engine was a necessity on a cruising sailboat. Expensive, dirty, malodorous, demanding, and troublesome, but necessary all the same. My conversion did not start to manifest itself in really concrete ways until a long-ago summer morning at Monhegan Island.

I had a nice little sloop then, a real little "go anywhere" type double-ender, and like everybody else I had an engine, in this case a little one-lunger diesel manufactured by a Scandinavian firm of high repute.

Thumper (as I called her for obvious reasons) and I never got along very well together. At her very best this creature would chug along, sounding as though a strong man was down in the bilges pounding away with a sledgehammer. With the noise came serious vibration and the vile stench of burning diesel fuel in large doses. The boat would, I must admit, then move along at a useful six knots.

But this was only when the motor was at her best. "Her best" seldom lasted more than a day or two after leaving the boatyard where I stored her over the winter. As soon as that expensive place was a few days behind us, old Thumper would begin to demonstrate her true nature.

Starting was the big problem. She really did not care to do it.

The starter would crank and crank and crank until after many, many long minutes, the frightful banging down in the hold might reluctantly commence, or, just as likely, the battery would run down to a point where it just gave up. Even if there had been room to try the hand crank, which there wasn't, such an effort would have been laughable.

Thumper, I came to realize, was an evil reincarnation of that old nemesis the Water Bitch. Disgustingly, she was a substance abuser, too. Given measured doses of ether at starting time, she would sometimes feign friendliness and cooperation, but this was false and treacherous playacting. You could never really count on her.

As time went on, I became progressively less reliant on Thumper and when, on that long-ago morning at Monhegan, the reincarnated Bitch made her definitive spiteful statement by breaking her own crankshaft, I was ready.

Hardened and weaned by a device that had tormented and ultimately betrayed me, I was now more than ready to give engineless cruising a try. No repairs, and no more ether for Old Thumper.

The rest of that summer was a time of discovery and unalloyed pleasure. Above all, there was a heightened sense of adventure. Every day on the water unfolded like a good novel with unexpected twists and turns, and a conclusion that never revealed itself until the very end. If I had a particular destination in mind, I might not get there, but along Maine's island-and-harbor-dotted coast, I invariably got somewhere just as good.

I found that fears of running out of wind and being left to endure long nights of helpless drifting were greatly exaggerated. Patience when becalmed seemed always to be rewarded by an eventual saving breeze. I found that every moment of my time on the water had become more intense, more interesting, and far more enjoyable. New kinds of experience were part of the reward.

I remember a day quite a few years ago when *Penelope* and I were becalmed in a thick of fog for many long hours off the eastern shore of Vinalhaven. It was one of those days when the forestay is only dimly and intermittently visible in the all-encompassing vapor. There was no sound, and the water was as flat and glassy as a mirror, so there was little or no motion, either.

After hours of this, the effect can become a little like what is described in accounts of sensory deprivation experiments. Deprived of external input, the mind works overtime and perception is altered. Then, too, the very nature of fog can change what we hear and see.

A white and Day-Glo red lobster buoy appeared to port. The shape was right, but the thing looked as big as a boat. Others, just beyond it, glowing in a dazzling array of Easter egg colors, seemed supernaturally bright and as big as houses.

Then I became aware of very faint music. It was a tinkling sound a bit like crystal glasses shattering in the far distance, but there were harp notes and chords in it, too, an ethereal melody with no probable source I could think of.

This unearthly music grew louder and came closer and closer.

Whatever was out there kept coming straight for me. The music was ever louder, overwhelming now, beautiful and thrilling, but terrifying, too. I didn't know whether to expect an angel or an alien spaceship to emerge from the fog.

Then I saw a faint dimpling on the water, and felt the first warm, gentle droplets on my skin as rain swept my way out of the mist. In seconds what had been a gentle shower became a deluge, and I dove below where I listened to the rain thundering on the deck overhead, drums now having taken over from the harps and triangles.

In a few minutes it was over and I emerged to see a faint sun overhead and the barely discernible spruce-studded outline of Vinalhaven over to the west. A seal peeked at me from a few yards off, then dove. I could see him swimming under the boat, a graceful green form in the green water.

All that happened many years ago, but I remember it like it was yesterday, a magical morning I will never forget. If I'd had a motor, I would have been using it, chugging along toward the Fox Island Thoroughfare, cursing the rain and breathing diesel fumes. The seal would never have come anywhere near, and I never would have heard the music.

2. Servicing the Mooring

A bright still morning in late June. Half tide. These are the conditions I have been waiting for in order to service my mooring for the coming season. It has to be calm so there is little risk of swamping my minimal dinghy while I work.

Half tide is ideal because there will be enough slack in the rode so that I can get a substantial section up into the boat for cleaning without having to lift the heavy chain off the bottom. Since it is only the upper portion of the line (the part nearest the sun) that accumulates weed, there is no need to clean any lower.

Less than half tide and I would risk not being able to get back to shore over the rapidly emerging mudflats.

I capture my English setter Sparky and shut her in the house over vociferous protest. She likes to assist me in all my projects, but her presence can be problematic around boats and mud.

Now I pick up a spar buoy and the pendant from last year and head for the dinghy. I am also carrying a dull kitchen knife, which will be used to cut and scrape kelp and other growth from the rode. Dull is good because while the knife will easily cut through stems and strands, and scrape off mussels, it will not damage the nylon and Dacron of the lines.

The descent to the shore is steep and uneven and, due to the fact that I recently tore a ligament in my knee, a little painful and uncertain. As I dodder downward I reflect that age is catching up with me, and I wonder how long I will be able to do these things.

I reach shore in company with a swarm of deerflies. Our part of Maine is not really suitable for civilized habitation until sometime in early July when, for some reason, these creatures moderate their behavior. Today I know I am going to lose some blood as I alternately row and swat on the way out to the mooring.

Getting to the large white ball, I realize I am not going to be able to get it into the boat while seated on the thwart. The ball is too big for me to get my arms around it without leaning perilously out over the water and inviting capsize. I will, however, be able to get it aboard by kneeling in the bottom and bringing the ball in over the transom.

Sounds straightforward enough, but with the knee and a certain amount of stiffness that comes along in bigger doses every year with our move to Maine, it is not so easy. I find that I am whimpering and groaning, and talking to myself while doing these simple things.

The ball comes in and I get to work with the knife. The ball itself is relatively clean and I reflect that it would have picked up more growth in a week down in the Low Country of South Carolina where we winter than it has over a whole season here in Maine.

Now I start hauling in rode and cleaning it. Here the growth is pretty impressive. Long fronds of kelp come up, their roots straining to penetrate and disrupt the strands of the line. I pull at some of them, but they are pretty tough when dealt with that way. The knife is the answer.

Along with the kelp are green weed, hairy fiber, worms, and mussels. A crab falls into the bilge along with a baby eel. I was always taught that eels are born in the Sargasso Sea and make their way here after a long and arduous journey. It seems hardly credible that this tiny, fragile creature could have made that epic trip, but I know he did. Very carefully, I scoop him up and drop him back in the harbor. Such a miraculous voyager deserves consideration and respect.

The rode is clean now, but the dinghy is a real mess. Full of crud. I am covered with it, too, and I smell like the sea bottom.

I bend on the pendant with a bowline and a hitch (I know, I know, should be an anchor hitch, but somehow I never learned to tie one). Then I use a rolling hitch to connect the spar buoy with the pendant and the job is done!

Since I am on the water anyway, I don't go home right away, but head out into the harbor. I may not be able to walk very well these days, but I can still row, and it feels good to work the muscles in my arms and back.

A light south wind is riffling the water, which sparkles and dances. And it brings the fresh scent of the sea from over Harbor Island. There is a tang of spruce in the air, too. My heart leaps, and I realize I am as happy as I ever get. There is a whole summer of this ahead.

3. The Way the Wind Blows

When I saddle up *Penelope* I rarely venture to say where I am going. Such a statement would be pure speculation, a kind of wistful expression of hope. No, I like to keep my options open. The idea is to take advantage of changing conditions, and follow whatever intriguing path opens up. As much as possible, I like to cooperate with the elements, not fight them.

Beating out the Western Way from Burnt Coat Harbor, Swan's Island, I take note that a massive fog bank is rolling in from the sea and will be on us within moments. A slight chill comes with the fog as it wraps around us. The lighthouse astern and Gooseberry Island to starboard disappear, as does can number 3 close by . . . and everything else. It's eerily quiet, too. Nothing to be heard but the muffled lapping of wavelets against the hull and the occasional distant cry of a gull.

The breeze is such that we can just make a course for a waypoint in our GPS that will keep us clear of rocks off Gooseberry Island, and in the vicinity of the High Sheriff before slacking the sheet and bearing off on a more northerly course up Toothacher Bay. This heads us for a new waypoint that will allow us to clear the north end

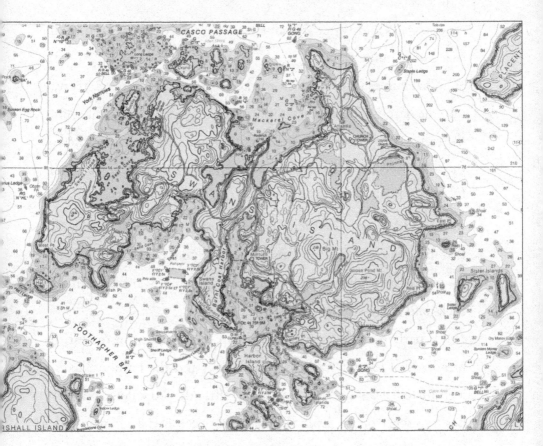

of Marshall Island and then head west between Marshall and the Halibut Rocks for Merchants Row and beyond—or, alternatively, north for the York Narrows and points east.

The upper levels of the fog bank thin as we proceed up the bay. Looking straight up, I can see blue sky, but at the surface and up to a point just above the tip of our mast the fog stays as thick as ever. The result is strange and wonderful. The fog on the water is transformed into a golden gas, and the chill departs as we float in a warm golden world. We ease ahead, gently captured in a dream-like trance. I'm reminded of the paintings of Maxfield Parrish, and almost expect to see swans and water nymphs weaving and dancing among the swirls of coppery vapor.

What comes instead is a sturdy ketch chugging along on her way into the harbor. She appears dimly in the mist and passes quite close, the reek of her diesel momentarily overwhelming the clean smell of the sea. Waves are exchanged, but the waves from the ketch are half-hearted. Her crew peers grimly forward. They look tense and worried, and I feel sorry for them because they don't seem to be enjoying this magical morning. Perhaps they are relying on dead reckoning, in which case a measure of concern is certainly warranted in this rock- and ledge-strewn place.

Or perhaps they are afraid their prop will catch on one of the hundreds of lobster warps between them and the harbor. That's a legitimate fear, too. *Penelope* with her smooth, propellerless bottom has no such worries. Even the notch between her skeg and rudder has been bridged over so there is nothing to catch on underwater lines.

Somewhere around the north end of Marshall Island, *Penelope* sails out of the fog into a clear sunny day. Spruce-crowned shores of unforgiving granite and basalt are once again clearly visible, and we can give the GPS a rest. Now it is time to think about where we may be going. A glance to the north reveals that the Casco Passage and York Narrows are shrouded in fog, so an eastward adventure is out unless we want to desert this delicious sunny morning and plunge into the mists again. More attractive are the sparkling waters that lie to the west over Isle au Haut way. That island rises majestically from the sea, a uniquely high blue-gray silhouette beyond and behind the low green form of Marshall.

We haven't been to Eely Oley, as some folks call her (the computerized voice of NOAA weather gives the name its best shot with *Eel Eee Hot*), in a couple of years, and it is always a pleasant place to visit. Due to a rather tenuous connection with the mainland, "progress" has not intruded too markedly and it is easy enough to imagine you have traveled back a way in time. There is a handy store not far from the landing, and good hiking, too, so in my dual capacity as captain and crew I unanimously pass a motion to make this our goal for today.

Penelope frolics westward until we have the grassy, treeless mound of Southern Mark Island close abeam. Gulls cry and squabble on shore, and rows of shags silently spread their wings to dry in the sun. The sharp smell of guano drifts over the water, seasoning the breeze much in the way a bit of anchovy will add depth and interest to a good beef stew.

Now we discern a softening around the edges of our lofty destination ahead. The outline becomes indistinct as another big fog bank boils in from seaward and threatens to engulf the whole of Isle au Haut in a dank, dark cloud.

A glance over my shoulder reveals that the York Narrows and Casco Passage are now clear. The GPS does not declare RECALCULATING in this circumstance, but the flesh-and-blood instrument inside my head does, and I begin to think about Sawyer's Cove, a charming little gunkhole near Pretty Marsh Harbor on the west side of Mount Desert. Famed naval historian Samuel Eliot Morrison chose the spot for his summer home, and I've never had any trouble figuring out why.

The prevailing southwest breeze and an incoming tide promise an easy sleigh ride through the passage and on across Blue Hill Bay to the cove. One of the joys of single-handed sailing is the perpetual seamless harmony that reigns on board; skipper and crew are once again in perfect accord, so we jibe her over and head northeast.

Running up the bay, we realize we are on a converging course with a handsome wooden ketch of somewhere around thirty feet on deck. She is moving along at an impressive rate and I observe unhappily that she is going considerably faster than we are. Other boats are not supposed to have their way with *Penelope* quite so easily.

But then I detect a telltale spurt and burble of water at her stern and realize she is motoring. Honor is saved. I call over to ask what she is, and get back that she is an H-28. All sparkling brightwork

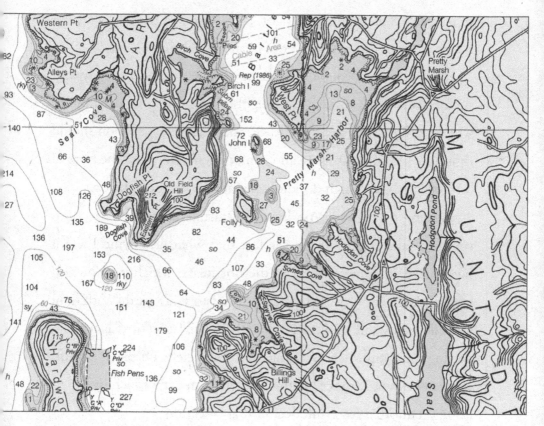

and clean white paint, she is certainly a lovely sight, and I say so. She cuts her engine and it is a treat to sail along in company for a while. Then the breeze begins to fail and the iron wind comes to life again on the H-28. She forges ahead and leaves *Penelope* bobbing in her wake.

We arrive at the passage and ghost through with an assist from about half a knot of current. With so little wind now we think about calling it a day and heading into Buckle Harbor, which is just to the south. It's a lovely, well-sheltered spot with extra-good holding ground and no human habitation or other works of man anywhere to be seen. When the tide is right, it's also one of the few spots left where you can gather a dinner of fresh mussels in no time.

Alas, there are a couple of large powerboats in there already, and such craft seldom make good neighbors. In quiet, isolated places where starlight, the scent of spruce, and the cry of the loon should rightfully prevail, the drone and stink of generators and the glare of TV reflected from high deckhouse windows just don't belong.

Pushing on between Asa Island to starboard and Black to port, we must take cognizance of the fact that what little wind there is has started to come around to the northeast, which puts our intended destination of Pretty Marsh dead to windward. With light and contrary wind, and tidal currents that will soon turn against us, getting there anywhere near nightfall is unlikely. Displaying a fine sense of humor, Mother Nature has added an extra touch by generating yet another fog bank over in that direction.

With the northeast breeze strengthening, I have a new idea. Back to the west we will go, only this time on the north side of the passage, close by Black and Opeechee Islands. Once through there it is only a short hop across Jericho Bay and into the Eggemoggin Reach, where there are any number of good places to anchor for the night. The anchorage off WoodenBoat Inc. in Brooklin, Center Harbor, and the Benjamin River all offer attractions; for that matter, you can anchor almost anywhere along the shores of the entire reach where the depths are suitable and the holding ground is good.

Now, as we run westward for the reach, the wind quits altogether.

We are in a narrow place between Opeechee Island and some ledges to the south. It is not a good place to be with no wind and becomes less so when I glance to the north and see distant lightning and anvil-shaped clouds coming our way.

As I await developments, I notice a large powerboat of the type locally known as a picnic boat bearing down on us from the west. A kind of elegant yacht on lobster boat lines, these have long been popular in the watering holes of the rich like Northeast and Southwest Harbors. Of late they have become ever bigger and sleeker, morphing from stately wooden craft in which a properly attired gentry would visit some uninhabited spot for a wholesome family picnic, to streamlined, jet-driven, fiberglass monsters, more on the lines of what L. Francis Herreshoff used to call "screwsers."

This one was running at around twenty-five knots and, as he approached, it was clear he wasn't going to slow down. Dead in the water, I could only watch him come and wonder how close he would cut it. Pretty close indeed. *Penelope* practically stood on end in his massive wake. Gear crashed above and below, and I could hear things breaking in the cabin.

I lurched up in the cockpit and roared out something very rude, which they no doubt could not hear over the whine of their machinery. This roar of rage was accompanied by a gesture, equally rude, whose meaning, I'm sure, did make it across the water. The skipper, up forward in his sleek wheelhouse, never looked in my direction, but his young and attractive female companion who was sitting aft in the cockpit surely did. She looked quite dismayed, terrified even. I hoped I had helped her understand what an idiot her boyfriend was, but more likely she was just aghast at the kind of foaming-at-the-mouth, obscenely gesturing old savages you could encounter while out for a innocent day afloat.

As the picnic boat quickly dwindled to a speck on the horizon and *Penelope* settled back down, we started moving westward again. Our following breeze was reviving nicely. Meanwhile the ominous thunderheads to the north seemed stationary. Squalls were howling, lightning bolts were raining down, and hail was crashing, but not, I'm happy to say, on us.

We reached the anchorage off the WoodenBoat School at an hour or so before sunset and decided that we had had enough for one day. Ignoring a whole raft of mooring buoys marked GUEST we anchored outside the mooring area in about twenty feet at low water. During a previous visit to WoodenBoat I had been disappointed to learn that "guest" doesn't mean "guest" at all, but "rental." Pick up the "guest" mooring and they hit you for fifteen dollars in the morning. Somebody should tell them there is a difference.

I was letting out some more scope on my anchor when a nastily pitched voice came from somewhere behind me, braying, "Hey you! Don't you know that you can't anchor here?" I looked back over my shoulder only to see my friend John from Swan's Island in a dinghy nearby having a good laugh at my expense.

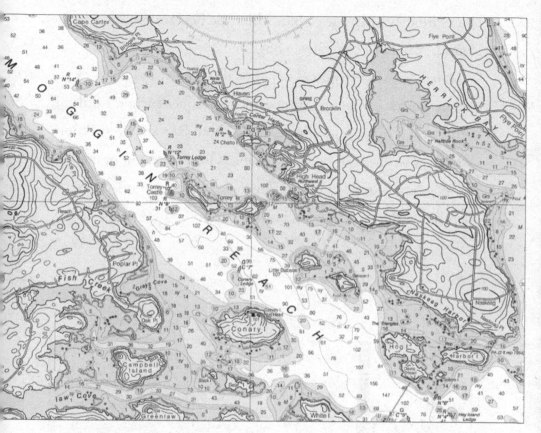

John and his bride of a year or so were going to get a ride to an inn in Brooklin and have dinner there. I thought of joining them, but as a heavy fog again rolled in off the reach, I thought better of it. Anchored quite a way offshore, it would be difficult to find *Penelope* later in zero visibility. Mellowed by good food and drink, I would have to row out into the swirling mists . . . No, I'd done it many times before, but it was never a very good idea. Besides, I hadn't been out long enough to miss shore food and human company. Steak, fried potatoes, and green peas topped off with some good Côtes du Rhône would do just fine on board; and jazz and blues from WERU out of Blue Hill, "the best radio station in the world," would be company enough.

It had been a pretty good day after all. Cradled and lulled by the gentle dances *Penelope* is performing around her anchor, I drift off into sweet dreams. All of the reach and both East and West Penob-scot Bays lie ahead or do, that is, unless for one reason or another *Penelope* and I decide to go off in some other direction. It will all depend on the way the wind blows.

4. Penelope Gets
a Fortieth Birthday Present

Increasingly in the summer of 2008 as we cruised among the islands, I began to notice that we had a problem with a very basic piece of equipment. After forty years of faithful service, *Penelope*'s wheel was showing signs of age. A certain relaxation had set into all its joints and, unlike its owner who has become increasingly stiff with the passage of years, it was becoming ever more flexible. Our once stern and rigid helm was metamorphosing into something better described as a floppy disk.

This yielding, almost malleable quality could be unnerving at times. Beating into a crowded harbor got to be even more thrilling than usual. A fresh breeze and you are close-hauled passing just to leeward of a moored gold-plater, cocktail party in full swing in her cockpit. A gust heels you over and weather helm comes on strong as you force the wheel over to stop her from rounding up and forcefully joining the festivities just to windward . . . What, you are compelled to wonder at such times, would happen if your creaky, floppy old wheel should choose just that moment to disintegrate in your hands?

Thoughts such as those coupled with the realization that, now into her forty-first year, *Penelope* was due for a belated fortieth birthday present led to the decision that a new wheel was in order. But then the problem was finding a wheel worthy of the occasion. A search of the usual marine suppliers and the Internet did not at first produce anything to my liking. What I really wanted was a nineteenth-century cast-iron job like what you would find on a schooner, a Friendship sloop, or a catboat in the golden age of working sail. Like antique chess sets, although there were millions of them, they are now very hard to find.

I was about to give up and accept one of the serviceable but less-than-wonderful modern substitutes when I remembered the Lunenburg Foundry up in Nova Scotia. Back in the days when the Grand Banks schooners ruled the eastern fisheries, the foundry was the principal supplier of all things nautical. Some years back when I had plans to put a make-and-break one-lunger into a gunning dory, I had seen their catalog. At that time it was still full of gear from an earlier age—make-and-breaks, manual windlasses, navigation lights, and, of course, wheels, wheels, wheels.

The 2008 version of their catalog when I finally got to it online was not quite the same. Much of the great old stuff was gone, notably the wonderful Atlantic one-lungers, but they still made mention of their traditional wheels. I could get the pattern I wanted, and if it was no longer available in cast iron, well then, sniff, I would just have to make do with bronze.

Custom-made with *Penelope*'s name and hail port cast right in, they could promise delivery in six weeks. The price, I admit, did give me pause, but on reflection seemed more reasonable. I had a quote from a local sail maker for a six-foot-five-inch bunk cushion that didn't come in at much less and, in that light, a one-of-a-kind bronze wheel began to sound like a steal. How many things can you own that are unique, beautiful, and, barring catastrophe, will last forever? The eight hundred bucks my custom wheel would set me back would be well spent and, unlike the money itself, represent a lasting treasure.

The Lunenburg Foundry did deliver in exactly six weeks and I can report that *Penelope* is very happy with her new wheel, as am I. She lets me bring it home to Vermont winters so I can look at it and dream of August sails. But about now (April) she wants it back so we can share it for another summer.

5. Oyster Run

Pulpit Rock both marks and conceals the entrance to beautiful Pulpit Harbor on North Haven Island. Just a morning's sail across West Penobscot Bay from Camden, the rock is crowned by an imposing osprey nest said to have been handed down from generation to generation of an osprey family for more than 150 years.

Along shore the once thriving canneries and lobster pounds have given way to the summer abodes of affluent but low-key rusticators. This is a good thing or not, depending on how you look at it, but everyone can agree the place is still one of the best and pleasantest harbors on the coast, with handsome farmhouses situated on rolling green fields that run down to the water's edge on the east side, and

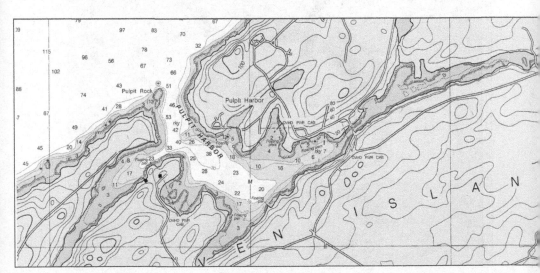

spruce-clad hills to the west.

An excellent store is about a mile's walk from the town dock, or, if you have a reasonably important shopping list, you can call the store and arrange to be picked up and delivered back to your dinghy free of charge.

Should you be having problems with your boat, a call to the delightfully old-fashioned Brown's Boatyard in the nearby town of North Haven will bring help. Old-fashioned in terms of aspect, manners, courtesy, and pricing, this is a wonderful yard to deal with.

If you are lucky, help will come in the form of Foy Brown himself. Master boatbuilder, master mechanic, raconteur, and one of the great characters on the Maine coast, Foy usually shows up in an old skiff with his grandson and his dog. A visit from this trio is not to be forgotten. If you appreciate sly, understated Maine humor of the kind that was more prevalent a few decades ago, you are likely to be royally entertained. Meanwhile, whatever your problem, Foy will fix it, and the price will be right.

Stepping ashore at the public dock in Pulpit Harbor and walking along the road a way, visitors will encounter the first of a cryptic series of signs that say simply OYSTERS with an arrow pointing on up the road. "Oysters what?" the uninitiated might ask. It's a little like the part in *Alice in Wonderland* where she finds a sign that says EAT ME, or maybe it's more like finding a jelly bean trail in the woods that will lead either to hidden treasure or to an evil witch.

In any case, if, curious and intrigued, you follow the arrows, you will eventually arrive at the home of Adam and Mickey Campbell and their oyster farm on a brackish pond not far from the harbor. No witches here. Try one or two of their exquisite mollusks and you will be hooked for good. Such was my experience quite a few years ago, and I've been coming back ever since.

Once or twice a summer *Penelope* and I make the always eventful passage from home on Swan's Island to the north shore of North Haven, Pulpit Harbor, and the oysters. Friends here on Swan's Island have become aware of this activity and I now receive commissions to buy oysters for them also. The oyster runs have become a tradition while *Penelope*, in a small way, has become an oyster freighter. I like to think she may now be the only craft on the coast engaged in interisland trade under pure sail.

A sunny August afternoon not long ago saw *Penelope* and your narrator headed out of Burnt Coat Harbor on another single-handed oyster expedition. Clearing the harbor and heading up Jericho Bay, I was happy to note that we were enjoying a fresh breeze out of the south. Going west as we hoped to be doing for the rest of the day would be a lot easier and faster than it would be if we had to deal with the usual sou'wester. My wife had rightly insisted that I pay some bills and mow the lawn before any gleeful escapes from the cares and responsibilities that plague us even on a remote Maine island, so it was already after 1 p.m. I had some ground to cover.

West past the Halibut Rocks we went, past Southern Mark Island, McGlathery, Round, Wreck, and the rest of Merchants Row. By the time we were level with Farrel Island it was after three and we had to decide whether to push on across East Penobscot Bay for some harbor on Vinalhaven or North Haven or to seek shelter on this side of the bay.

On an engineless boat there comes a time every afternoon when you have to decide whether to trust the breeze to get you where you

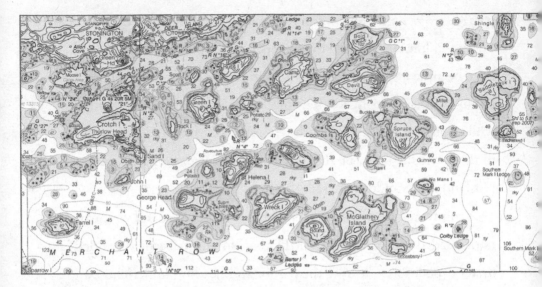

want to go or call it quits for the day. This is particularly true if pushing on involves passage over a large body of water. The risk, of course, is that the wind will die when you are out in the middle and leave you with an anxious wait for new developments. Much as I like being on the water, helpless all-night drifts do not rate among my favorite pastimes.

This breeze seemed stalwart enough and was, in fact, strengthening, so we decided to carry on. It was also true that the coming night's forecast called not for calm but for southwest breezes gusting to twenty-five or thirty knots. Under such conditions, no possible harbor could be better than Carver's Cove right at the eastern end of the Fox Island Thoroughfare, and this was where we decided we wanted to go.

Nearby Seal Bay, long a favorite of ours, would have been good, too, but ever since *Reeds Nautical Almanac* cited the place as one of the most beautiful on the coast it has become way too crowded, and the beauty, much of which had to do with pristine solitude, has become more difficult to enjoy.

Jumping off from the vicinity of Scraggy Island and the Brown Cow, rocky sentinels off the west side of Deer Isle, we have a straight shot for the Fox Island Thoroughfare, which lies just about due west. It's breezing up to well over fifteen knots and the silvery breaking waves are bathed in a copper-toned, late-afternoon haze. We are flirting with the time when reefing would be in order, but with the sheet slightly eased *Penelope* likes it fine and flies westward.

Scudding by Widow Island and into Carver's Cove, we pass a twenty-six-foot sloop anchored just outside, the only place in the immediate area that offers little protection from the prevailing weather. She is rolling uncomfortably in the chop and flying a yellow flag from her starboard spreader that looks for all the world like a quarantine flag. If she has come from some foreign port and is hoping to clear customs here, she will have a very, very long wait. The nearest port of entry is many miles away at Belfast.

I give up trying to figure out what she is and what she is doing out in the wind and chop. It's nice to see another small boat out cruising (a rare sight these days) even if her skipper doesn't seem to know what he is doing.

A whole squadron of Cape Dory boats are already lying in the anchorage—an association cruise I guess—but there's plenty of room for everybody in this commodious place.

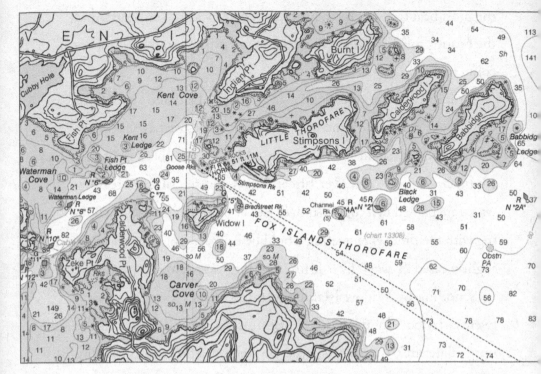

With the anchor down and the boat all squared away, I bring out the TracFone and attempt to phone my wife. It's no go, though, just as it has been at so many anchorages this summer. Cell phone service along the coast seems to wax and wane from year to year, and this year is a bad one.

Four or five years ago I could connect from almost anywhere. Now attempts to use the phone are met with the NO NETWORK message nine times out of ten. Sometimes you can go ashore and climb a high hill to try to get results, or sail out into open water. Sometimes it works, usually not.

A while later a large and powerful-looking Winthrop Warner sloop, all fresh paint and bright varnish, comes in to add a little vintage class to the assemblage. In a conversation next day her proud owner mentions that her current condition is the result of a three-year restoration project, "24/7." I believe him and am full of admiration for the dedication involved. Thoughts of my own maintenance program, which is restricted to one afternoon every spring when I paint the bottom and the trim, leave me feeling suitably humble.

I have brought a couple of fresh haddock fillets from home, and sautéed in olive oil along with a little Cajun rub they go down very nicely. A couple of glasses of a nice Chardonnay join the mix, along with some great blues music from WERU in Blue Hill.

The evening is passing very pleasantly. Short of a working telephone, I can't think of anything I need or want. We are snugly sheltered by the nearby shore and even the presence of the recently constructed giant wind turbines—which now loom over the anchorage like alien invaders from *The War of the Worlds*—does not bother us much.

Monday morning arrives with the same stiff breeze and a thick o' fog. I can just make out the quarantine-flagged boat out in the wind and the chop. He has moved and contrived to anchor in an even worse place. Maybe she is a real plague ship, I think, or maybe her skipper is doing some kind of penance. He sure looks like he is making things as hard on himself as possible.

The wind and the fog do not promise much for an early start so I decide on a leisurely breakfast of steak, eggs, and home fries. This, as usual, is a great success. Part of my reason for cruising is how really wonderful even the simplest food tastes when out on the water.

Some of the room left over from when I took the engine out of *Penelope* now goes to house a Weber Baby gas grill. We keep a folding bicycle and a case of wine down there, too.

The grill is ballast most of the time, and only comes out early in cruises when we still have fresh meat. Later the Origo pressureless alcohol stove takes over and our cuisine goes downhill somewhat, descending from fresh fish, grilled chicken, and steak to Spam, corned beef hash, and other items of that ilk. Amazingly mealtimes are about equally eagerly anticipated and enjoyed during both stages of a cruise.

Breakfast over, I'm ready for some exercise. For starters, I row over to the largest of the Cape Dories to see if his cell phone works any better than mine. The answer is no. The skipper says the farther Down East he gets, the more worthless his phone becomes. I'm tempted to say that the farther west I get, the more the same thing happens, but don't.

The skipper then suggests that I try the marine operator by VHF. This is not very helpful because the marine operator is only a distant memory. The last one gave up a few years ago, back when cell phones really worked out here.

Now I take a long row around the anchorage, starting slow and winding up hard and fast. You get plenty of exercise cruising an engineless catboat, but not much of it is aerobic. Rowing fills this gap, and I love to do it anyway.

Along the way I pause by a seining dory moored offshore that has become headquarters for a raucous band of terns. They are using the old boat as headquarters for their acrobatic forays in search of food. Camera always close at hand, I have been hoping for a chance to get some good shots of these elegant fliers.

They let me get pretty close, and one pair in particular intrigues me. The one I assume to be the male sits on the stem looking grumpy while the female circles and darts overhead showering down a torrent of imprecation, instruction, and criticism. Reminds me a little of certain moments at home.

Back alongside *Penelope*, I notice that we have a stowaway. A large and truculent-looking praying mantis is crouching on deck. He is a lovely shade of green, and looks right at home, though his perch on deck is surely precarious. How he got there is a mystery because at anchor, moored, or under way, *Penelope* has not been close to shore for months. When I set my camera case on deck a few feet from him he panics and takes off over the briny deep.

Bad move. He is not a very accomplished aviator and his flight path soon veers to port and downward with a soggy impact on the crest of a wave.

Not overly given to sentimentality, I nonetheless feel responsible for this creature's plight. He was on my boat after all, and however unintentionally I scared him off it. Now I row over to where he is and get an oar blade under him. He gets the idea quickly and grabs on.

He is in the dinghy with me and I head for shore. He regards me from the stern sheets, then, not done with his ill-advised attempts at aviation, he launches himself forward and lands in my beard. A bit panicked myself, I shake my head violently and he falls off into the bilge, where once again he sloshes around on his back. This is not going well for either of us.

I can't remember stuff I once knew about praying mantises. Can they bite? Do they latch onto you with those formidable-looking mandibles and not let go? I don't think so, but I'm not sure, and I don't want to find out the hard way. I decide to let him be where he is while I row as fast as I can to shore. I'm not offering any more rides in my beard.

Touching shore at last, I offer him the oar blade again and he climbs on. I lay the oar blade on the transom, and now only a six-

or eight-inch jump will land him safely on shore. Alas, his leap falls an inch or two short of that modest goal. Now he is the plaything of the waves washing up on shore. First he is carried up and he grasps for solid ground, but then the backwash gets him and he is carried back out into deeper water.

This happens over and over and he is beginning to look more than a little bedraggled. The dinghy is caught in the same wave action and I'm afraid we will crush him as we crash back and forth against the beach. Finally a wave sends him careening against a rock that is high enough to be dry on top. The mantis grabs a strand of rockweed and climbs wearily to the summit. The tide is going down so if he bides his time a little, he will be able to step off onto the beach unscathed.

I take this as my cue to depart. My karmic duties have been fulfilled. He is now in a better situation than when I found him. I wish him well and head back for my boat.

But now, of course, he is likely to step ashore and meet some fetching mantis lass. She will show him a nicely formed mandible, and one thing will lead to another. A part of mantis lore I do remember is that just when he reaches the pinnacle of all his ambitions with her, she will bite off his head and that will be the end of his story. Well, I can't do anything about that.

The fog is lifting and the wind is falling light. I decide to take advantage of what is left of the breeze and head onward for Pulpit Harbor. We sail off the anchor and head back into East Penobscot Bay.

Leaving Carver's Cove bound for Pulpit Harbor, we have a choice of going around North Haven either clockwise (west about) or counterclockwise (east about), approximately the same distance either way. An easy decision because the first part of the counterclockwise route will be downwind. In an engineless boat, you always take downwind when you can get it. Hardy, moralistic types who choose to do the hard part first frequently find that the wind will shift at some time during the day, and suddenly they have the hard part last as well as first.

Running out of the anchorage, *Penelope* seems to be going about as fast as the light following breeze. Although we are moving along at a good three or four knots it seems airless and the sun is getting very hot. I can't feel the wind on the back of my neck or judge its direction by turning my head and determining which ear is getting more. There are only the ripples on the water to tell me this.

I don't mind the heat, and this easy ghosting along is delightful. But our peaceful idyll is shattered by the attack of a squadron of monster green flies.

Bloodlusting, dagger-jawed demons, they attack in fast, low-flying swarms, circling and diving to deliver their stinging bite. And when they bite you really know it.

The battle rages. I'm reminded of old newsreel footage of 1940s naval battles in the Pacific. Dive-bombers and massive antiaircraft fire. Flak-filled skies, ships burning and trailing smoke. I'm bitten a few times and manage to kill several of my attackers. It's not easy. You have to finish them off after you knock them down or they will revive and return to the attack. I smash the fallen with any hard object that comes to hand and toss them overboard.

Damaged but undaunted, we draw away from shore. The attacks diminish then stop altogether. We are off Babbidge Island now and look back to get a last glimpse of the turbines looming over Carver's Cove. Don Quixote would have picked up his lance and headed back, but we have other business and head north up the bay.

Off Sheep Island, which we are rounding to begin our passage along the north shore of North Haven, I can see that while we are enjoying a lovely breeze out in East Penobscot Bay, the water beyond Sheep is still and glassy. Off to the west it is dead calm as far as the eye can see. I think about staying out in East Penobscot and changing our destination to, say, Castine up the bay where the wind is still blowing. This would be the sensible windjammer's approach but we can't be sensible. This is the Oyster Run. We have to get to Pulpit Harbor.

So out of the sparkling breeze-livened water and into the dead, glassy calm we go.

We have Oak Island to starboard now and, not only is the wind gone, but the current is running against us, too. Pointed west we are in a race with a lobster buoy and losing. We are losing our race with Oak Island, too, as it draws slowly farther ahead.

About now the windjammer *Heritage* appears out of the west, pushed along by her yawl boat. Built relatively recently expressly for the windjammer trade, this large cream-colored schooner is one of the two or three loveliest boats on the coast.

As she passes, *Penelope* loses all steerageway and falls off until she is pointed back east and drifting along beside *Heritage*. The man at the wheel gives a thumbs-up and calls out, "Nice." Evidently he likes small gaff-rigged catboats because he has complimented us before in previous encounters. We, needless to say, are delighted with recognition from such a source.

A feeble zephyr now springs up out of the northwest and we are able to begin progress along the North Haven shore, albeit very slowly. A quarter of a knot against the tide is not much, but at least we are moving. I reflect that most of the north shore of North Haven, but especially this stretch around Oak Island and Webster Head, is frequently a dead spot. Of the many times I have been becalmed, or struggled along in very light air, a disproportionate number have occurred right here. There are a few such places along the coast, and the engineless sailor knows them all by heart.

West, out beyond Webster Head, wavelets have begun catching the sun. Countless jewel-like points of light shimmer, presaging the coming of the afternoon sou'wester. We inch along toward this welcome sight until, finally, we begin to feel a weight of wind.

Now we have a robust full-sail breeze and *Penelope* leans into it, making up for lost time as we tack along shore. A helicopter circles overhead. Emblazoned across its side are the words BOATPIX.COM so I guess we are having our portrait made.

A red lobster boat is working off the entrance to Pulpit Harbor.

As we tack shoreward there seems to be a continuing conflict of interest between *Penelope* and this boat. Wherever I want to go, she seems to be also going, and vice versa. It's almost comical how often our courses converge, he heading for yet another lobster pot, and I trying to make the best course to windward. Of course I do what I can to stay out of a working boat's way, but we seem to have an almost magnetic attraction for each other.

Past Pulpit Rock now, and entering the harbor proper, I decide to hang a right and go up into Minister's Cove. This little gut is mostly used by a contingent of Cabots who own summer houses along the eastern shore, but beyond their moorings there is plenty of room for a catboat to anchor, and the setting is far more tranquil than the busy and popular main harbor.

I'm close-hauled and driving at six knots toward a rocky shore—only yards away now. I must tack immediately, but I sense more than see that my friend the red lobster boat will be directly in my path when I do.

I've got no choice. I give a frantic arm signal to indicate the direction I must go and put the helm over. Collision seems more likely than not, and one thing you surely want to avoid along the Maine coast is running into a lobster boat. It just isn't done.

As I come up into the eye of the wind I hear a couple of loud crashes from the direction of my dinghy . . .

Now, lobstermen have various attitudes toward recreational sailors. Some tolerate them as an unavoidable irritation like flies or mosquitoes. Some actually like or appreciate them, especially if they have beautiful boats and handle them in a seaman-like fashion. Others are downright hostile, seeing them as a summertime plague that comes along every year like the red tide, feckless strangers from "away" with too much money and too much leisure. The fact that summer sailors have been known to become entangled with and destroy a lobsterman's hard-won gear doesn't help the situation.

I had encountered all these attitudes at one time or another, but I had never so enraged a lobsterman that he would physically attack my boat. But this is what I feared was happening now.

Then a voice rang out. "There's some dinner for ya." Looking back into my dinghy, I see that what has crashed into it is a fine pair of lobsters. Over on the red boat I can now make out the smiling face of Adam Campbell, lobsterman and oyster farmer extraordinaire.

"All right!" I call out. "Thank you." Then *Penelope* is almost on top of the other shore in that narrow entryway, and it's time to tack again, and away.

We made our way through the Cabot fleet and found a quiet pool beyond the mooring field. Anchor down, we would just have time to cook our lobsters before the onset of mosquito hour.

Anchored farther up in the shoal water near the head of the cove was a small pulling boat covered by a tent-like canopy made from a blue plastic tarp. Somewhere around thirteen feet long, she looked like an Iain Oughtred–designed Scandinavian faering I had seen in *WoodenBoat* magazine: a beautiful craft, but very small. I could just make out a bearded face visible in an opening in the canopy.

Now, here was a true minimal cruiser. Sailing as I do in a small engineless catboat, I am usually the resident minimalist in any anchorage I visit, but this guy made me look like J. P. Morgan. I determined that I really wanted to talk to this fellow, find out how his cruise was working out and where he was going. But that would have to be for tomorrow. There wasn't time to cook and go visiting before the mosquitoes made their nightly visit.

I tried phoning my wife again but that of course was hopeless. Then I tried phoning Adam Campbell or his wife, Mickey, to order up a load of oysters to be picked up next day at the town dock, but here at North Haven I couldn't even reach a number on the same island.

A voice was drifting over from the minimalist cruiser. Who could he be talking to? I couldn't believe there was yet another person on that tiny boat. It just boggled the mind. Perhaps his cell phone worked better than mine, or perhaps he was just talking to himself. All single-handed voyagers are a little crazy, and many of them talk to themselves from time to time. I do it myself.

That settled, I got down to cooking my lobsters. Sadly I didn't have any butter to melt, but olive oil in which a little garlic had been sautéed did well enough. There was chilled white wine, and as usual WERU came through with some good jazz. We settled into a tranquil and pleasurable evening as the stars began to wheel overhead. It's a hard life, but somebody has to do it.

Tuesday morning sees us up with the sun—around 5:30 a.m. I am really looking forward to a chat with the minimalist in the faering, but a look up the cove reveals that he has already departed. I wonder if he has left so early because he likes to take advantage of

the morning calm for his epic rows, or if the morning version of mosquito hour drove him out.

His canopy looked equal to any rain that might come up, and he did seem to have some kind of screening, but my own experience with makeshift screens and tents leaves me believing that the bugs always get in anyway. Sadly the details of his voyage and his beautiful little boat will remain a mystery.

I have half a lobster left over from last night, and this along with some bread and mayonnaise will be breakfast. I can't help thinking a little smugly that my breakfast will be better than that of the departed minimalist. Something tells me that his breakfast was more like the ones that Scott and Helen Nearing used to offer the young idealists who came to help them with farmwork.

I can see the volunteers coming down on the first morning, visions of blueberry pancakes, home fries, bacon, and eggs—a real hearty "Good Life" farmworker breakfast—dancing in their heads. In the dining hall, the Nearings would offer them a cup of water, a handful of whole grains, and a mortar and pestle in which to grind them up . . . Bon appétit!

Many minimalist voyagers for some reason seem to be minimalist eaters and imbibers, too—traits, I hasten to add, that I do not share.

I get in the dinghy and begin the long row to the town dock. From there I cross the bridge and climb the long hill that leads to the island store. It's worth noting that the island store is at Pulpit Harbor, not in the town of North Haven where you would expect it to be. There used to be a great old-fashioned grocery and butcher shop in North Haven called Waterman's, but that is another story. Old Mr. Waterman would cut you a really nice steak if he wasn't off to play golf with some summer people.

At the store I find a kind of raised platform, possibly used for unloading trucks. I clamber up on this (note that I have already climbed a substantial hill) and, holding the TracFone high above my head, dial my home number. A tinny, computerized voice tells me that if I want to use the such-and-such network I must dial the whole ten-digit number, complete with area code.

This I duly do and, wonder of wonders, I can hear my home phone ringing. Then my answering machine comes on and my own voice, the last thing I want to hear, tells me to leave a message. I manage to get out, "Hi, sweetie, I'm at Pulpit Harbor," when the phone goes dead, and no amount of leaping in the air and holding the phone aloft will bring it back to life again. At least my wife will know I'm still alive, and that comforting thought will have to do her for now.

I punch in the Campbells' number and am delighted to find that not only does the phone work in this context, but one of these busy people is at home. I quickly arrange with Mickey Campbell to meet at the town dock where she will deliver my order of oysters. I then repair to the store and buy a twelve-pack of Coors just to make the walk back to the dock more burdensome.

I'm back at the boat by noon with my beer and my cargo of oysters. No wind is stirring so I get out my deluxe antigravity chair and a book and while away an hour or so, waiting for wind. Around one o'clock there is a stirring from the west, and soon there is a pleasant five or six knots from that direction.

I waste no time in getting sail on her, and the anchor up, heading out. As I retrieve the anchor, the rode sticks in the bow roller where a shackle joins chain to nylon line. Perhaps unwisely I decide to sail out that way and deal with the problem when we reach more open water.

Approaching Pulpit Rock and running before the pleasant little breeze, we notice that despite our efforts to steer away from it, *Penelope* seems intent on running right up on the rock. It is only by sheeting in the sail that we can make her sheer off, away from danger.

About now a Herreshoff Bullseye comes sailing merrily by and leaves *Penelope* like she was standing still. Now we know something is seriously wrong. Bullseyes just don't sail by *Penelope*.

I heave to and go forward to find that my dangling anchor has snagged a lobster pot and has been dragging it out of the harbor. This explains the steering problems and how the Bullseye could leave us in the dust. I free the lobster pot and finish retrieving the anchor. Then we are off after the Bullseye, just to show who is really boss. They aren't having any, though, and quickly turn around, coming back in our direction. Ah well.

Down by Webster Head we run out of wind again. Same old dead spot. We lie drifting in circles. Time passes and the sweltering heat and the flies that always come off the land to greet you when the wind dies are becoming onerous. Finally the water to the west begins to darken, showing that wind is on its way.

It's five in the afternoon by the time we are off Crotch Island and Stonington, but we now have a full-sail following breeze. Once again we have to decide to trust the wind or prudently call it a day. This breeze is high cotton for our intended route, so we sail on by McGlathery Island, the last useful anchorage along our way, and head for home.

Penelope flies along this familiar route and we are having a great time. The current is somewhat against us and will be more so—dead on, in fact—when we reach Jericho Bay, but with this much wind it doesn't matter. We can give back a couple and still make almost five knots over the ground.

As we pass the Halibut Rocks, the breeze begins to slacken. It is falling away just when we need it most. With an incoming tide I realize I must sail for a point way west of Hockamock Head and hope that we can weather the line of ledges and rocks that make out from there and lead into Burnt Coat Harbor.

The wind dies altogether when we are off the High Sheriff. Forward progress ceases and we begin drifting backward.

There is nothing for it. Out come the oars, a nice pair of long sculls that used to propel an Alden Ocean Shell. Hockamock Head with its lighthouse and the harbor entrance is visible a little over two nautical miles to the east. To get there we must skirt the aforementioned rocks and ledges for most of that distance, leaving them to port and downcurrent.

Progress is painfully slow. I seem to be making half or more like a quarter of a knot in the direction I want to go, which is crabwise across and somewhat against the current. There is some residual chop, too, which slows the boat and rocks it, causing the boom to bang into my head if I don't duck repeatedly as I stand to the oars. My friends the flies and mosquitoes are back in force and I am defenseless against them, my hands tied up with the sculls.

We gauge our forward progress by our relationship with nearby lobster buoys and learn that, at our present rate, we are going to be out here a long time. Tedium, frustration, and discomfort reign for what seems like eternity then disappear for good when I happen to look over my shoulder and see massive black thunderheads massing to the north.

We may be tired, arm-weary, insect-bitten, and sore, but we are no longer bored. Our new emotion is not exactly fear, but could be called healthy apprehension. I've been rowing for an hour now and have made maybe a third of the distance I need to get into the harbor. The light is failing fast, partly due to the time of day, and partly due to the boiling jet-black clouds that have begun to cover the sky.

Conditions are dramatic to say the least. This looks like it could be a serious storm. Very heavy weather is a real possibility. If I had sea room I would consider dousing the sail before it, but here, with rocks and ledges close by on many sides, I would lose steerage and all control. Ending the cruise on a rocky shore would be the almost inevitable result.

Nothing to do but press on and hope for the best with lightning slashing down to port, and thunder, a sound like distant warfare, getting closer.

I feel the start of a breeze now, and quickly stow the oars below. We begin sailing, the squall hits, *Penelope* staggers under the blow, and then we are almost literally flying. I've gone over seven knots a couple of times before in this boat, and I know we are doing so now. Fortunately we are running before it with the harbor dead in our sights.

The day has gone pitch black and the thunder and lightning come from overhead, flooding our surroundings in garish staccato flashes of blue-white light and bursts of crashing sonic mayhem. I'm fleetingly reminded of the strobe-lit discotheques we sometimes frequented back in the 1960s and '70s. The lighting is right, but even their high-decibel pandemonium would seem hushed and sedate compared with this.

We shoot in past the lighthouse as heavy rain begins to fall. I steer to port and we gain the welcome lee of Hockamock Head.

There is no telling if the worst is over or if the fun is just beginning. I heave to and anchor immediately. I have no thought of trying to find my own mooring up at the head of the harbor, no thought of trying to reach home and a hot meal.

Right now I just want to sleep.

6. Teaser-Breezer

Those amusing fellows at NOAA-nothing (the National Oceanic and Atmospheric Administration) had predicted west winds of five to ten knots. Now, we are not so naive that we actually expected a breeze from the west. Long experience had taught us better.

On the other hand we have not fallen so far from the turnip wagon that we could not muster some hope that there would be a breeze of some sort; any direction would do.

NOAA has this part down pretty well. Usually, when they say there will be wind, there will be. The direction from which it comes is another matter. And if they say "light and variable" the engineless sailor should definitely stay at home.

On this particular day an early-morning west wind duly made an appearance, wafting along at a delicious eight knots. Losing no time we quickly sailed off our anchor and headed out into Blue Hill Bay from Mackerel Cove, Swan's Island, where we had spent the night.

Well, our lovely little breeze turned out to be what we call a teaser-breezer. No sooner did we reach the red-and-white bell at the eastern end of the Casco Passage than it shut down completely. Through the long morning hours we drifted helplessly. First one way, then another, but always within sight of the bell.

Afternoon came with no change. A minuscule zephyr would waft us a few hundred yards in one direction until its opposite sprang up and wafted us back to our starting point, always within sight of the bell. We sat out there for eight hours until around 4 p.m., when the lightest of zephyrs came along and persisted in a feeble sort of way.

It was not enough to keep the sail full as the boom rocked with the gentle swell, but it was enough to keep sail and boom mostly to port, where the sail would belly out briefly at intervals, before the boom rocked back a little and the sail collapsed.

Thus propelled we were able to maintain what I estimate to be one-eighth to one-quarter of a knot back in the direction from which we had come. Two or three more hours of this found us back at our original anchorage where I thankfully called it a day. Thank you, amusing fellows from NOAA-nothing, for another great day on the water.

7. Encounter at Orcutt Harbor; or, The Noisy Neighbors

It was late, and as *Penelope* ghosted north along the Cape Rosier shore in a dying breeze, we decided we'd better head into Orcutt Harbor, a deep gut running up between the cape and Condon Point. It was that or nearby Buck's Harbor, picturesque but always much too crowded for my taste.

I'm not in love with Orcutt Harbor, either, because way up at the head of the harbor where it is shoal enough for comfortable anchoring, it tends to be quite buggy. Or, to put it more bluntly, I've found more mosquitoes there than anywhere else on the Maine coast. The engineless sailor must take what he needs when he can get it, though, and with the wind dying and the sun going down, there wasn't much choice.

As the harbor opened up before me, I was distressed to see not one but four or five truly monstrous powerboats in there. The kind that look like pocket ocean liners and can only be owned by the super rich. The late Aristotle Onassis used to entertain Maria Callas and Jackie Kennedy on one. His archrival Niarchos had one, too.

This alien presence was a big surprise because to quote from Taft and Rindlaub's *Cruising Guide to the Maine Coast*, Orcutt Harbor is

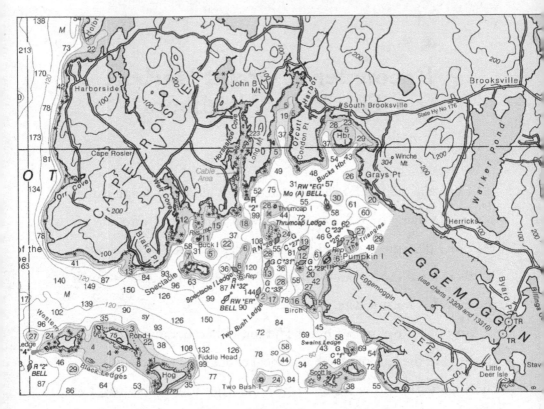

normally "little used by yachtsmen."

The big boats were clustered approximately halfway up the harbor, which meant that by proceeding all the way up to mosquito headquarters, I could put at least half a mile between *Penelope* and them. Mosquitoes are onerous, but I much prefer them to the all-night drone of generators and air conditioners and the attendant diesel fumes. Some of us cruise to get away from the more decadent aspects of modern civilization; others, it seems, will go to any expense to bring it all with them.

The mosquitoes were happy to greet us, and due to the late hour were out in force. Getting the anchor down, the sail furled, and all the other chores attendant on anchoring were accompanied by a lot of swatting and slapping and not a little foul language.

I was kneeling on the foredeck enveloped in a cloud of stinging insects and just clipping on a twenty-five-pound sentinel (a weight that is lowered partway down the anchor line to form a catenary and ease strain on ground tackle) when, KA BOOM! one of the behemoths downharbor fired off a signal canon. A real mega blast to match the mega yachts.

A seal who had been lolling on his back and regarding me from quite close by practically exploded in fright, and a loon who'd been cruising around a little farther off dove for China. I hit the deck like a ton of bricks (reflexes picked up in Vietnam die hard) and, most irritatingly, dropped my very useful sentinel. It hit the water with a mellow *kerplash* and went to join the old soup cans and wine bottles that litter the bottom of every harbor.

I've always wondered why certain individuals and organizations find it necessary to shatter the peace of waterborne evenings in remote settings with massive explosions at sunset. Perhaps they do it for the visually impaired who otherwise might not know that night was on its way.

Sans sentinel and full of sentiments less than benign, I spent the rest of the evening battling mosquitoes and missing a hot dinner because I don't like to cook with the boat all buttoned up. Sardines and Fig Newtons were a poor substitute for my planned steak and baked beans.

Morning came glorious and bright, as only a Maine morning along the coast can. The new day was full of promise, and the unpleasantness of the preceding evening receded quickly to the realm of distant memory.

Eight a.m. saw me leaning over the side rinsing out the spider after breakfast ("spider": a large cast-iron frying pan). BROOOOONGH!!!!! One of my massive neighbors downharbor cut loose with a mighty horn blast, surely louder than anything the *Titanic* or the *Queen Mary* could ever produce.

Well, you guessed it, the old vet hit the deck again, and, oh no!, the spider made a hardy splash as it went to join the sentinel and the old soup cans. Disaster. I can't cruise without a spider. I cook in it and eat out of it. It is more important, probably, than the compass.

Now really, would you come into any other neighborhood in the world on a peaceful morning when people are just waking up, or perhaps enjoying a quiet cup of coffee in the sunny morning stillness, and unleash the sonic equivalent of an atomic bomb? No, you wouldn't. It's just not good manners.

The mighty horn blast from the mega yacht might at least have been expected to signify something, but, in fact, it had no discernible effect. No one hauled anchor and left, no one on any of the boats out there even came on deck. Nothing happened at all.

It seemed more like a declaration. Something like: "Behold! My name is Ozymandias, King of Kings: Look on my works, ye mighty, and despair!"

Well, I didn't despair, though I was greatly saddened by the loss of my sentinel and my spider. I just got out of there as soon as there was some wind.

Got motors?

8. Anchoring and a Good Night's Sleep

There are only two kinds of cruiser—those who have dragged anchor, and those who are going to. In northern waters this is just a fact of life. There are so many things that can go wrong with a single anchor dropped into the obscurity of an unseen and unknown bottom that failure and the dreaded involuntary trip to leeward and potential disaster are bound to occur sooner or later. In tropic waters where you can swim down to see how your anchor is situated you are somewhat ahead of the game, but plenty of dragging goes on down south, too.

The whole issue of anchoring and dragging can be avoided, as so many modern cruisers seem to do, by only stopping in places where rental moorings are available and paying for the somewhat dubious security of lying on someone else's mooring. But this precludes enjoying most of the more secluded, charming, and beautiful anchorages along our coast. And I'm old enough to think the usual fee is more appropriate to renting a full-service motel room than simply picking up a string tied to a rock.

We won't even talk about marina slips. My attitude in that regard is amply illustrated by the fact that in over sixty years of cruising, I have never used one.

What can, and does, go wrong with your anchor when the worst happens? Let me tell you a few stories . . .

My wife and I were anchored at Nantucket sometime back in the 1970s when a full-scale gale arrived one evening. Our twenty-one-foot sloop rode to her twenty-pound CQR all night without incident. By morning the breeze had diminished to around thirty knots and, having already weathered much worse, we were not expecting any problems.

It was with some surprise, therefore, that we found our morning coffee interrupted by the sight of moving masts and boats all around us. But it was not other boats that were moving so rapidly upwind, it was us, hellbent for destruction in the opposite direction. Letting out what little scope we had in reserve did nothing to stop us, but fortunately the kedge was ready to hand, and it saved the day.

Retrieving the CQR taught me a valuable lesson. Lodged on the tip of the plow was a rusty old soup can, and its simple presence had rendered our otherwise trusty anchor about as effective as a bowling ball. Since we had ridden all night in winds of forty-five to fifty knots, I figured the anchor must have worked very slowly backward during the night—it could have been as little as a few inches—until it found the soup can in the morning and we started our sleigh ride to shore.

When you consider that every harbor known to man probably has at least a million soup cans strewn around its bottom, not to mention old buckets, broken bottles, and other debris, you realize you can never be absolutely safe from a similar occurrence.

Anchored at a then very remote and uninhabited cay in the beautiful archipelago just south of Warderick Wells in the Exumas, I had an almost identical experience only this time the culprit was a small conch shell. Not to be outdone, the Maine coast provided me with a dragging episode at Roque Island via whelk shell, and another in nearby Bunker Hole where my anchor became fouled in heavy kelp.

At Spanish Cay in the Abacos, Seal Bay in Vinalhaven, and the Barred Islands in East Penobscot Bay, anchors of ample size deployed at recommended scope have failed simply because the bottom was too hard or too soft, and the wind and wave action were heavy.

In one case I believe an anchor failed simply because the rode was too thick and strong! This was a case of a small boat with a light but appropriate anchor. The rode was a very heavy one from a much larger boat. With ten-to-one scope but in a high wind with a vicious chop, the anchor was yanked clean out of the bottom. A thinner rode with more stretch would have greatly reduced the strain on that anchor, and, so eased, it most likely would have held. In this regard, it should be noted that a "sentinel," a weight suspended partway down your rode, forms a catenary, and makes a great shock absorber in all such cases.

Through the years, it can be seen, I've had my share of difficulties with anchors and anchoring, but all this hard-earned experience brings with it a certain expertise, or so I thought. A sort of I've-seen-it-all kind of thinking creeps in. At its worst it can lead to overconfidence.

Thus I was almost grateful for a new lesson this past summer. I found that although by now I know all about soup cans, conchs, whelks, gobs of fishnet, and kelp, there are still surprises down there and I will probably never know all of it.

Penelope found herself anchored between Round and McGlathery Islands in Merchants Row off Deer Isle one August night. Following my usual practice for engineless anchoring, I had reached toward my chosen spot then let go the sheet and dropped the hook. The anchor hits bottom while the boat still has some way on, and this momentum is used to set the hook. She then rounds up and you drop the sail. This method of setting the anchor is about as good as backing down under power but perhaps not quite. In any case, if you don't have power it's the best you can do.

The night passed without incident, but hauling anchor in the morning I realized something was wrong. The anchor seemed about four times heavier than normal. When it finally broke the surface I could see that a large spruce branch was lodged in the elbow of the CQR. Heavy enough to make it feel like the anchor had set; light enough to have caused real trouble if there had been any wind in the night.

Just one more story along these lines: I remember a brisk Maine morning a few years ago when suddenly I found myself beam to the weather and drifting rapidly toward shore. This time a rush to the anchor line and a hard yank yielded no answering pressure at all. The line, when it came in, was heavily abraded in one place and completely severed in another. This was not in some coral-infested tropical gunkhole but a well-known and popular Maine anchorage.

Faced with so many unknown and unknowable hazards, how is the anchoring cruiser to get any sleep? You may remember the song from the musical *Cabaret* about "two ladies." Well, my song is about two anchors. Granted it's something of a pain in the derriere, but setting two anchors before you go off to dreamland will obviate almost any chance of involuntary and potentially disastrous journeys in the night. This of course applies only to known anchorages with decent holding ground. If you are over thick kelp or ledge, ten anchors won't hold you.

My ideal pairing is a CQR of ample size and a "fisherman" or "yachtsman" of equally generous proportions. The CQR is an excellent anchor and, used alone, is one of the best, most versatile and reliable patterns going. But the fisherman is also excellent and, undeniably, will hold in places where the CQR will not, while the reverse is not true.

The fisherman leaves much to be desired when used alone, however, because if wind or tide causes the boat to sail around or over the anchor, the rode is very likely to foul the exposed fluke, at which point holding power goes from very high to close to zero. In tandem, though, and set far enough apart so the boat can't drift over the fisherman, these two anchors are unbeatable. None of the various anchor problems described in the earlier part of this article is remotely likely to happen to both of them at once so, unless the sea gods are really out to get you, you should get a good night's sleep.

9. What Grandma Told Me About Catboats

When I was five years old my father and I went to visit G. Frank Carter, the well-known boatbuilder, in his boat shop on a marshy creek running up into the village of East Quogue, Long Island. I don't remember much about that day except that Uncle Frank's workplace smelled great. (Proust can have his madeleines; I'll take fresh cedar shavings and marine varnish any day.) And you could see water through his floorboards. Then there was a SINCLAIR OIL sign with a big green dinosaur on it that I really liked a lot.

Even then it was clear to me that Uncle Frank had a situation and a way of life to be envied. I could tell that my father held Uncle Frank in something like awe, and it was impressed on my young mind that the boats there were something very special.

He was "Uncle," by the way, because just about all male members of our family were called "Uncle" this or "Uncle" that. I think that in those less mobile times when many of your neighbors and associates were also relatives, uncles were a more prevalent species, even when they weren't really uncles.

My grandmother and her sister Minerva, for example, used to call their brother "Uncle Willy" and he was just plain "Uncle" to everybody else. We had plenty of "Aunts" too. Uncle Frank was in fact my grandmother's first cousin, and he was known far and wide for the beautiful catboats he produced year after year.

Decades after this early visit, shortly after my return from Vietnam, I took my new fiancée on a nostalgic tour of my childhood haunts around the shores of Shinnecock Bay. Driving through East Quogue on the Montauk Highway, I happened to look off to my right up a narrow creek, and there was Uncle Frank's boat shop, still there and still in business. A sign along the highway advertised—as it had for well over half a century—SAILBOATS FOR RENT. The whole scene, the ramshackle sheds on pilings, the graceful boats from another era, the lazy creek with its cattails and nattering mallards, seemed a dream-like vision from another time.

G. Frank, of course, was long gone, having been at least eighty on my previous visit. The current proprietor was aged about right to be a grandson or a nephew. Having said I wanted to rent a sailboat, I was subjected to the rigorous examination all would-be charterers must face. "Well, fella, know how to sail?"

"Yup" was the right answer, and I had qualified. "Take this one," he said. It seemed incredible that you could so casually get your hands on a craft that would more fittingly be on display at the Smithsonian. But, actually, it wasn't quite that easy.

"This one" turned out to be not one of G. Frank's white-and-buff swans but a slightly ugly duckling of turquoise hue, which I was somewhat aggressively informed was "of my own build." It was becoming clear that this latter-day Carter chafed at living in the shadow of his illustrious ancestor and longed to be recognized for creations of his own.

The turquoise-colored number "of my own build" was an okay boat, just a bit crude in relation to the real thing. The joinery was not nearly as good, and the lines, while pleasing, lacked the magical perfection for which G. Frank was known. The color . . . well, let's just say that it lacked gravitas. She sailed well enough, though, and my fiancée and I had a fine day aboard, scudding over the shallow flats, stopping for swims and a picnic.

We got as far as the Ponquogue Bridge in Hampton Bays and then returned to East Quogue in the late afternoon. Going back, we sailed close to the South Shore and got a good look at the Caffrey House where my grandmother and her brothers and sisters grew up. The familiar complex stood back from the bay on a low bluff, partly hidden by a row of ancient cedar trees. It looked pretty much unchanged from the way it was during my childhood, unchanged even from when my grandmother was a girl.

My grandmother was born Florence Caffrey on September 19, 1883. She grew up on that neck of Shinnecock Bay known as Tiana Bay in the heyday of the catboat. Across the bay to the east was an area known as the Ram Pasture, and beyond that the now demolished Shinnecock Light.

Grandma had a lot of things to tell me about catboats and other subjects we don't hear so much about today. I remember fascinating excursions we would make into the countryside. One favorite was along the then still-extant five-mile path through pine and oak woods she had taken to and from school as a girl.

Grandma could name every plant and tree along the way and tell you what they were good for. She could point to where hundred-year-old wells lay hidden under the blueberry bushes and tell how they had been made by sinking an oak barrel into the low, sandy soil. She knew all the insects, beneficial and otherwise, and could tell you what kind of wild ducks and shorebirds were flying when, to me, they were only dark specks in the sky. She could also point out what was wrong when some summer person was making a bad job of sailing along in the bay.

My grandmother's parents, Emmaline (née Squires) and John

John and Emmaline Caffrey and offspring.

Caffrey, ran the Caffrey House, a large boarding establishment that took summer guests from New York City. It was very much a family business and my grandmother, with her sisters Minerva and Mary and her brothers Frank and Willy, worked long hours along with their parents.

The Caffrey House and several other large shingled or clapboard frame structures dotted this part of the Shinnecock Shore. There were several imposing private houses along with the Pine Grove House run by Aunt Alice, who represented another branch of the family. At any distance from shore, human habitation pretty much ceased. Civilization gave way to vast stretches of pine woods and scrub oak, broken occasionally by a potato farm or a small village like East Quogue or Good Ground (the present-day Hampton Bays).

Most of the buildings along shore sat back from crumbling sand banks that led down to the shore below where graceful open catboats rode on their moorings or lay alongside the long wooden docks that extended as much as fifty or sixty yards into the shallow bay. There was a peaceful, sheltered quality to this soft mix of land and seascape quite different from what I would get used to and come to love so many years later on the coast of Maine, but of course you didn't have to go very far—just across the bay and the dunes beyond—to find the old Atlantic in all its wild majesty.

Guests at the Caffrey House were mostly couples and families. The women and children tended to stay for long periods of time in the summer while the husbands worked in the city during the week

A Charming Cool Summer Home

The
Caffrey
House

East Quogue
Long Island

BOATING

SAILING

BATHING

ROWING

Pleasant Rooms - Good Food

Reasonable Rates

and came out to enjoy the shore on weekends. The same people returned year after year. In many cases they considered themselves, and were considered, as something like family. But if there was affection or even love between the family and some of the guests it was never unmixed with a certain amused condescension also.

Men from the city were sadly inept at the manly arts of hunting,

The Caffrey House

EAST QUOGUE :: LONG ISLAND

Those who love water sports and who appreciate real American home cooking, are steady patrons of THE CAFFREY HOUSE, once they enter our home. As the picture shows, the house is on high ground, swept by cool bay breezes, assuring restful nights and happy days.

There is a clean, white sandy beach, where children may safely learn to swim, within sight and call from the piazza. Only a few minutes' drive to the Quogue Surf Bathing Pavilion, which is well equipped for bathers, or to Peconic Bay for still water bathing.

The wide, roomy piazza extends nearly around the house, affording shady spots all day. The house is on the edge of a pine woods, affording a pleasant walk, only a short way, to the Post Office.

The house is equipped with electric lights and inside toilets.

All vegetables grown on the place, fresh picked each morning. Home raised chickens. Club sailing races may be viewed from the house. Write for terms. Phone ~~Hampton Bays 4-M-)~~.

RA-8-4470

sailing, and fishing, and the women were delicate creatures who didn't understand real work. Not for them were the fourteen-hour days in the cook shed or laundry room where our own womenfolk seemed to derive a kind of cheerful rectitude. A man could be a successful doctor or lawyer, but if he couldn't tie a bowline or knock down a fast-flying sheldrake, there was something child-like and helpless about him, not fully deserving of respect.

Cooking at the Caffrey house was done in a long, narrow, low-ceilinged shed that featured a number of zinc-lined sinks on one side and four giant coal- and wood-burning stoves along the other. On hot August afternoons with all four stoves roaring, cooks and waitresses in a manic dance, dishes, pans, and screen doors slamming and clanging, that cook shed was quite a place.

Outside the shed there was a wood-plank walkway leading to the coal bins. One afternoon when I was ten years old my father showed me his name written on one of those planks with nails. He said he had written it there when he himself was ten.

Near the cook shed was the root cellar, which had a wonderful dank smell so pungent that it stung my young nose. There were various kinds of tubers in there but I remember mostly sweet potatoes, along with dairy products and eggs. Back a way from the waterfront and the main buildings was an extensive garden that produced corn, potatoes, cucumbers, squash, and fresh greens. Beside the garden were a pair of chicken houses that supplied Sunday dinner, a big event on the weekly calendar. The bay provided fresh fish, fluke and flounder mostly, along with hard-shell clams and blue-claw crabs. Clam fritters were a famous specialty of the house.

The main building, which contained more kitchen space, the dining room, a "lounge," and living quarters for the family, had previously been located across the bay on the dunes where the Shinnecock Inlet now runs in and out (before a storm broke through the dunes to create the inlet, the bay had been a brackish landlocked lake with a totally different ecology than it has now). The house had been the US Lifesaving Station for that part of the coast, and my great-grandfather Caffrey, an Orangeman from somewhere around Ulster, had made his way here to become chief of station, responsible for launching lifeboats into the stormy Atlantic to save shipwreck victims.

When the service was shut down, and its functions taken over by the Coast Guard, he loaded the building onto a barge and sailed it across the bay to where it became the Caffrey House.

Assisting in this mind-boggling adventure was his brother-in-law Fred Squires, a quintessential bayman and famous duck hunting guide of those times. Fred was the grandson of Ellis Squires, my great-great-great-grandfather, who with his father, mother, two brothers, and seven sisters sailed an open "ship's yawl boat" from Machais, Maine, to Goose Creek near the head of Peconic Bay in 1773, thus establishing the family on these more temperate and accommodating shores. It must have been a pleasant change from the harsher clime of eastern Maine, but this new paradise had its drawbacks. Wildfowl were so abundant then that people living near the shores of Shinnecock and Peconic Bays were kept awake nights by the loud honking and cries of geese and brant. It's ironic in a way that, dismayed by rampant development in our part of the South Shore of Long Island (among other things, the geese and brant are no longer there in any great numbers), I reversed the family's migration more than one hundred years later by sailing a twenty-one-foot sloop back east, and buying a house on Swan's Island.

When Fred Squires died in 1956 he was out clamming on a chill November day at the tender age of ninety-four. My father and Uncle Joe found him drifting in open water still clutching the inner tube that held a hard-earned bushel basket full of littlenecks and cherry-stones.

Fred left an estate worth 250,000 1956 dollars, not counting his waterfront home and land—which by the 1960s were worth several hundred thousand more—so you have to figure he guided a lot of duck hunters and dredged up a lot of clams and scallops in his day. It's interesting to note that never in the course of a very long and successful career did Fred ever get as far away as New York City, a mere ninety miles from home.

As a teenager, I tried commercial clamming myself for a few summers and was dismayed to find that success had a great deal more to do with skill and experience than youth and vigor. One day when I was fifteen, I went along on a clamming expedition with my father who was then in his forties, Uncle Willy in his sixties, and Fred who was over ninety.

Well, you guessed it, Uncle Fred who by that time had gone from being a normal-sized man to a tiny, bent, gnome-like creature, came in way ahead as to number of clams dug. Willy, who was a little frail to begin with, was second, my father third, and I, exhausted and blistered, a distant last.

My commercial clamming was carried out, if not from a classic Shinnecock Bay catboat, at least from a cat-rigged boat, which I felt was traditional and proper. When the bayman of old hunted, fished, scalloped, crabbed, or clammed, he did so from a catboat. With the advent of the outboard this sadly changed. Large flat-bottomed skiffs became the workboats of a new generation. But even in the late 1950s old-timers could still be seen working out of cut-down catboats. One or two retained mast and sails to save a little gas on the way home, or perhaps even to garner a little surreptitious pleasure from sailing.

My boat, the *Hasty Heart*, was a nine-foot sailing dinghy with an eighteen-foot mast, spreading an impressive sail area for her size. She was quite fast and truly exciting to sail. Formed out of two layers of molded mahogany plywood and finished bright, she was an attractive and able little craft, but perhaps due to her shape and color bore an unfortunate resemblance to her brand name, which was Kidney Boat. My bayman relatives thought this was hilarious and never let me forget my boat's association with the urinary tract.

Guests at the Caffrey House, for the most part, were lodged in the Annex, a massive two-story-plus-attic affair with a rocker-lined porch overlooking the bay. Accommodations were Spartan by today's standards. There was an iron bedstead in each room and a washstand bearing a large porcelain bowl and a pitcher kept full of cold water. Lighting was by kerosene lamp. I was going to say there was a communal bathroom down the hall but, on reflection, I'm not sure there was. Certainly there was no electricity and no hot water until 1947, when the area was electrified. One thing I do remember was a functioning four-holer out by the chicken houses.

The Annex, massive structure that it was, had been built single-handed by an Uncle Roger or Uncle Rogers, I'm not sure which, a feat that won him universal acclaim. Even in those days when they were so much better at handling heavy objects by simple means (think of boatyards before the advent of the travel lift and projects like getting the rambling old Caffrey House on and off a barge and up over the bluff behind which it now stands), feats like raising the ridgepole on a huge barn-like structure by oneself must have been, well, daunting.

On clear summer days the boarders were issued box lunches and in the late morning would stroll down to the dock where two or three open catboats waited. The men in their straw boaters and the women in their long skirts, white blouses, and large hats must have made quite an elegant assemblage.

The boats would take their passengers across the bay to the dunes and the ocean beach beyond. In the evening the process was reversed. On occasions when the wind died, the boatmen would row the couple of miles back to the main shore.

One day, while skippering one of these catboats, my grandmother's seventeen-year-old brother Frank slipped and fell against a cockpit combing. A couple of days later he was dead from internal injuries.

One August night shortly after the turn of the century, seven or eight of the local young people left shore in a twenty-one-foot catboat bound for a moonlight sail. It was a beautiful evening with a soft breeze and a star-studded sky. The next morning the boat was found drifting and empty. The bodies of the young people were found one by one later in the week.

Speculation at the time had it that someone got into trouble while swimming off the boat in a calm, and that one after another the others went overside to help. When they were all in the water, a breeze came up and wafted the boat away.

The Caffrey house still looks out over the bay, essentially unchanged behind its row of old cedars, but everything else is different. The woods and the sweet, fecund marshes are mostly gone, and so is the teeming wildlife that went with them. The whippoorwills that once filled summer nights with their electric call are gone forever, and the last box turtle was crushed under the wheels of a car many years ago. The elegant wooden boats are mostly gone, too, along with the people who had the taste and skill to build and use them. I was born a couple of generations too late to be there for the heyday of the catboat on the bay, but I miss it anyway.

The following is an excerpt from an obituary that appeared in the *New York Times*:

G. Frank Carter—Boatbuilder

1867–1961

A catboat designer and builder for more than 65 years, G. Frank Carter launched more than 150 beamy gaff-rigged cats from his small boat building shop behind his home on Wesuck Creek. In addition, he built another fifty boats, including sloops, small cruisers and runabouts. He built his sailboats in their entirety and made the sails himself. Even as a nonagenarian Carter personally test-sailed his new boats in nearby Shinnecock Bay. Mr. Carter observed on his 92nd birthday that he could, "just sit here at the house, rocking the time away, but I just don't see any reason to change after this many years at the shop."

10. Line Squall

The sudden squall, that explosive, dangerous blast of wind that comes seemingly out of nowhere, is a fact of life on the Maine coast. Such squalls are rare in summertime, but the possibility is always there, and the mariner should never forget it.

A few years ago a full-sized schooner in the windjammer trade was knocked down and sunk by one of these rogue winds near the Deer Isle Bridge in the Eggemoggin Reach. And in a race off Camden not so long ago, a large and expertly crewed Friendship sloop went down in the same way.

An August afternoon a few years back saw a line squall sweep much of the Maine coast. I experienced it in Blue Hill Bay, and a friend of mine tells me it hit him off Schoodic that same afternoon. The *Bangor Daily News* reported gusts of forty and forty-five knots, and noted that the storm thrashed boaters and knocked out power to sixty-two hundred homes. The following is an account of what it was like for *Penelope* and me.

Sometimes I can't help the feeling that the gods don't want me in Blue Hill Bay. From our home base on Swan's Island, the mid-Maine coast from Rockland to Schoodic has been a wonderful playground for more years than I care to count.

A vast and wonderful playground, that is, except for Blue Hill Bay. Every time *Penelope* and I head up that way, we get into some kind of trouble, usually having to do with too much wind. I keep trying, and it keeps happening.

Once I was up by Bartlett Island on my way to Blue Hill Harbor when a quickly building northwest breeze made it clear that it was time to reef. This I duly did, but then there was a sudden and complete lull. *Penelope* fell off until she was lying broadside to the direction from which the wind had come.

I was quite annoyed as we lay there to think that now I might have to reverse the tedious reefing process. Then, out of nowhere—WHAM!—we were struck broadside by a truly monumental blast. *Penelope* lay perilously far over as she tried to round up. Green water lapped high up on the lee cockpit combing, and water poured down through the clamshell vents on deck. If you know catboats you know this is not a recommended posture for them to be in. I thought sure the old girl was going to go over, but almost miraculously, she didn't. I scandalized the sail, and we fled south out of Blue Hill Bay.

This and a few other unpleasant Blue Hill Bay adventures were on my mind on another August day as, once again, we ventured north into what for us has always been a watery nemesis. Objectively, though, I knew the bay was much the same as any other place along this part of the coast, and damned if we were going to be put off by a run of bad luck and coincidence.

Evening found us in Sawyer Cove, a delightful little nook near Pretty Marsh Harbor on Mount Desert Island. Here we passed a pleasant night enjoying a brilliantly star-studded sky, and the eerie conversation of a pair of loons.

Next day the morning breezes were such that continuing on to Blue Hill Harbor would be a long beat against wind and tide. I decided to leave the town of Blue Hill for another day, preferring to run for the Eggemoggin Reach and points beyond in true windjammer fashion.

Penelope drove west around Tinker Island and ran up the Flye Point shore with the intention of going inside Sand Island and Channel Rock. When Sand Island came into view, however, I was unable to make out the nun that is supposed to lie just inside it. This was disturbing because there are more than a few hazards in the area, and it is certainly a place where the prudent mariner wants to make sure he has all his ducks in a row.

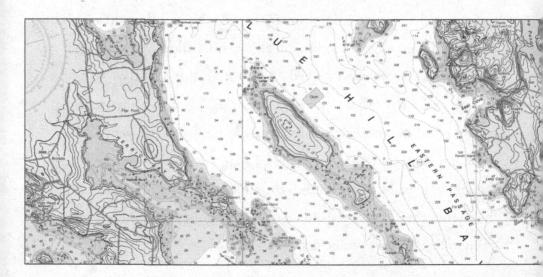

With my undivided attention on Sand Island ahead, I may have had less-than-normal awareness of what was going on around us. I did realize that the breeze was making up considerably and it was time to reef.

Consequently, I hove to on the starboard tack, swigged up the topping lift, and lowered the gaff to near horizontal in preparation for the process of reefing. Now we were broadside to the wind and headed toward shore, about three-quarters of a mile off. It was here, halfway into the reefing process, that I finally realized what was bearing down on us from windward.

A black sky and an angry phalanx of huge white horses were rushing toward us in a gray fury of driving rain. A totally different day from the sunny bluebird affair I had been enjoying, and could still see stretched out to the south. A different world. Recognition merged with actuality as *Penelope* was struck by a roaring wall of wind and water.

With the sail scandalized and the sheet eased, she was not in danger of capsize, but she was now driving toward shore at an alarming rate. I saw that the leech of the sail and the battens had wrapped themselves around the lee topping lift and were flogging and flapping with a sound like gunfire. I watched while the longest batten, the one about halfway up the leech, made a hole at the inner end of the batten pocket and shot right through the sail, flying arrow-like fifty or sixty feet from the boat and disappearing into the sea.

My options were not appealing. In our present configuration we would drive ashore in a few short minutes. Tangled as it was, getting the sail down altogether might, or more likely might not, be possible, but then we would have no control at all and would drift sideways into a line of rocks to port.

With the sail scandalized, coming about and heading away from shore was not a possibility. Peaking her up and trying to come about in this weight of wind did not recommend itself, either. Luffing, insofar as it was possible, aided the sail in its efforts to flog itself to death while only minimally slowing our headlong progress toward destruction on the rocky shore ahead. Finally the idea of wearing ship and trying to jibe her around, particularly with the sail all hung up in the rigging, looked like a surefire recipe for disaster. I felt the way the driver of an eighteen-wheeler must feel when he loses his brakes halfway down a long mountain descent.

I decided to wait until we reached more modest soundings, and then attempt to anchor. If the anchor held, we could probably round up and get the sail down. What followed would be uncomfortable, but at least we would still have a boat.

Just as I was about to crawl forward for the CQR on its roller, there was a relative lull. The wind dropped from around forty knots to maybe twenty. Without any conscious thought I found myself at the peak halyard, hauling like a demon. Up went the peak, in came the sheet, and we were coming about. As we went through stays, the wind speed reached back up toward its previous level.

Penelope sagged off a little, and we experienced a near knockdown similar to the one described earlier. Then my tough old girl fought her way back up and, by means of considerable luffing, we were able to get some sea room.

By the time we were over by Tinker Island, the wind had subsided again, down to about twenty knots. At that point we were able to tie in a reef and limp homeward.

Okay, gods, if you don't want me in Blue Hill Bay, I won't go there anymore.

11. Picking the Right Boat

I was twelve years old when my father decided it was time for me to have a boat of my own. A search of available and affordable craft in the East Quogue–Hampton Bays area finally narrowed down to two candidates. There was a tiny plywood hydroplane with a five-horsepower Evinrude, and there was an eight-foot sailing dinghy. Initially, I was all for the hydroplane. My visions of speed and glory far outstripped anything that ridiculously inappropriate little vessel could have provided. But, hey, I was a kid.

Fortunately my father knew better. He patiently explained to me that motorboats are essentially boring. Driving a motorboat, he said, was like driving a car, only you didn't even have to worry about keeping it on the road.

Sailing, on the other hand, was always full of interesting challenges. Getting the best out of a boat, and learning how to use wind and tide to achieve your objectives, was an endlessly fascinating quest that would last a lifetime.

I wasn't really convinced, but luckily I still had undiminished respect for my father's wisdom and other god-like qualities, and somewhat reluctantly opted for the sailing dinghy. This emerged as a major turning point in my life.

The hydroplane would have been a dead end, leading nowhere.

Hopelessly unseaworthy in anything but flat calms, it would have turned out to be a useless toy, and taught me nothing.

The *Hasty Heart*, as the little sailing dinghy became known, opened up a new world. During the long summers of my youth, I virtually lived on her. Days of sun, wind, salt spray, and rushing, pounding motion; nights at home in bed where it all happened over again as I still felt the surge and scend of the sea, and slept in a salt-encrusted, sunburnt dream. There isn't anything better.

Now in my mid-seventies, I can still manage to have those days and wave-tossed nights if I get up early enough, and sail long and hard enough, and there still is nothing I would rather do.

Hasty Heart, circa 1957.

12. Bottom Painting

For a couple of years during my late teens I had a summer job working at Sid Allen's boatyard, up a marshy creek in Hampton Bays, Long Island. Sid Allen had been a friend and close collaborator of Gar Wood, and at that time held the franchise for Shepard speedboats on eastern Long Island.

For somebody who had been associated with the quest for world records in high-speed motorboats, Sid sure had some strange ideas about engine care. He had a 1949 Ford station wagon with over two hundred thousand miles on it, and proudly claimed that he had never changed the oil. He did carry a five-gallon can of Wolf's Head motor oil in back, and from time to time would add a dollop to the gooey mess in the crankcase. That old Ford smoked a little, but always seemed reliable.

For a dollar an hour I did most of the jobs other workers didn't want any part of. Primary among these were bottom cleaning and bottom painting.

A boat would be hauled up on one of the marine railways, where it sat a scant two or three feet from the ground. My job was to get under the boat with a hose and a stiff broom, and use the sand that lay between the railway ties to brush and scrape barnacles and other marine growth from the bottom.

Lying on my back and scrubbing away at the surface over my head, I had a steady diet of copper paint chips and dust falling on and into my face, mouth, and nose. It was physically exhausting and generally pretty unpleasant. The only recompense was that all this happened around boats, and that seemed to be enough. I could have made more money stacking shelves at the A&P in Westhampton but to do so never occurred to me.

When the bottom was clean, painting was next. Lying in the same position and using old brushes no longer useful for more exacting jobs, I daily took on a layer of copper bottom paint as thick and seamless as any I was applying to the hulls over my head.

I have no idea how much bottom paint I ate, inhaled, and absorbed during those summer months, but it must have been a lot. I remember that I used to keep a shiny, mercury-coated quarter in my pocket in those days, too, and this, no doubt, added to my consumption of heavy metals. Ah well, we were young then, and there were not so many warnings on labels in those days.

These early experiences in bottom painting left me less than enthusiastic about the process, and when in later years I had boats of my own with bottoms that were supposed to be painted, I approached that task with something short of glee.

Penelope, who came to me only in my late fifties, got her bottom painted for a few years, but the job was even more unpleasant than it had been when I was a kid. A bad back made the required tasks almost unendurable.

Then I made a wonderful discovery. I had been painting the bottom with ablative paint, mostly because it was advertised that you could apply new coats without sanding the old ones. Ablative bottom paint is supposed to wear off as the season progresses, taking any accumulated marine growth with it as it goes. But the old coats do not wear off entirely and there is a buildup of paint as the years go by.

One November after hauling, as I finished power-washing the bottom, I realized it was still covered with many coats of now clean bottom paint. What would happen, I wondered, if next spring I just omitted bottom painting altogether?

I tried it and was delighted the following November to see that only a very thin layer of green slime had adhered here and there on the hull over the summer season—not much more, in fact, than if I had applied fresh paint in the spring.

It has been five years now since *Penelope*'s bottom has gotten anything more than a power wash, and the results are great. There has never been enough fouling to materially affect sailing performance, something that makes this old bottom painter very happy.

Note: This strategy, or lack thereof, is recommended only for chilly Maine waters.

13. Along the Reach

Monday, August 11, dawns gray and bleak. *Penelope* lies at anchor off the WoodenBoat School, near the eastern end of the Eggemoggin Reach. I down some coffee and scrambled eggs then row the dinghy in to the busy WoodenBoat School dock. The school runs various charters and sailing classes from here, and there is a constant PFD-clad procession going on and off dinghies and launches, headed out to and coming in from an assortment of handsome wooden sailing craft in the harbor. Notable among them are a couple of austerely beautiful Friendship sloops and a sleek Herreshoff ketch. Then there is a dazzling array of smaller, open sailing boats, all of them, of course, made out of wood.

Detail, Friendship sloop off WoodenBoat.

All this is a feast for the eyes and I am reminded of something I read somewhere to the effect that when the shape of boats was largely determined by the natural lines that could be bent into wood, almost all boats were beautiful. Only when the advent of plastics made it possible for man to build any shape he wanted did a lot of truly ugly boats began to appear.

I make my way along the dock, past the boathouse and up the gravel drive leading to the boatbuilding school and the WoodenBoat store. Along the way I pass a large group preparing to launch the sleek wood kayaks they have either built at the school or built at home using WoodenBoat plans. Judging by their gear, they are off for some kind of extensive cruise in company. There is a palpable air of excitement and anticipation here, and I admire their spirit in the face of the weather forecast, which is for rain, rain, and more rain.

A little farther along, a fellow is fiddling with the gear on an Iain Oughtred–designed "john dory." Since I had built one of these myself a few years back and sailed it extensively before getting involved with *Penelope*, I stop off here for some enthusiastic dory talk. The builder mentions that he finds his boat a bit tender and seems grateful when I mention that I'd had the same problem until I solved it with the addition of a lead pig wrapped in a towel and a couple of plastic jerricans full of seawater, which I used as movable ballast.

Continuing on, I reach the top of the hill and the WoodenBoat store, which is hard to pass up if you like boats. Here you can find one of the best selections of nautical books available anywhere as well as a very extensive collection of boat plans for the wooden boat builder. There is also a small selection of specialty tools, like caulking irons, which are hard to find elsewhere. This is great stuff, and always worth the visit. I try to ignore the rest of the merchandise, which is fancy, overpriced yachting wear and other frivolous and pricey souvenirs. But if selling this stuff helps support the beautiful boats in the harbor and the organization as a whole, I'm all for it.

Normally I do my part by buying lots of books, and I do so again on this morning. A treasury from the old *Rudder* magazine, an autobiography of somebody's life in schooners, an account of Nat Herreshoff and his last Cup defender . . . It goes on and on. I am putty in their hands. But given the current weather reports, I am likely to need lots of reading material aboard *Penelope*.

At the register I notice that it has started to drizzle outside. As usual the cashier is stuffing my numerous purchases into a paper bag. It seems odd that while every other bookshop in Maine uses plastic bags, the WoodenBoat store, a large proportion of whose customers come in by water, sticks to paper. I point out the problems inherent in rowing a batch of new books out to my boat in the rain and they eventually come up with a garbage bag.

As I head back down the gravel road to the dock, I note again how manicured and opulent the whole place seems. From the extensive park-like lawns to the impressive mansion where the magazine offices are, it is more like a modern corporate campus than anything else. And this, I suppose, is what it really is. I guess in my heart of hearts I would like it to be something simpler and not so slick, more along the lines of an old-fashioned boatyard. But whatever it looks like, classic boat aficionados have to be very glad that it exists.

Back on board *Penelope*, I have a short gam with an old boy who is sculling out to a wooden ketch at anchor nearby. He wants to know how I reach the end of *Penelope*'s boom, which extends a few feet out beyond the transom. I tell him that it is usually not necessary to do so as the reefing pendants are led inboard and can be handled from the cockpit. I do admit that I once lost a nice brass hurricane lantern while reaching way out to hang it from a hook at the very end, and he seems pleased with this proof that, just as he thought, my boom is too long, and continues on to his ketch with a contented look.

I get into my foul-weather gear and go forward to shorten up the scope on my anchor. My method of sailing off the anchor involves shortening up until you can just feel your length of chain start to lift off the bottom. Then raising sail with a lot of sheet let out and waiting until she swings over to the tack you want, then quickly hauling in the rest of the rode, which usually gets you off in your chosen direction.

But sometimes—perhaps one time out of fifty—the bottom is such that the anchor does not wait for you, but breaks free immediately. Then you must quickly let out scope again and start over. Or, if there is nothing in your way, you can simply pretend this was what you had planned all along and sail on while leisurely retrieving your anchor. Today was one of those one times in fifty, but there was nothing in our way so we sailed off looking very casual and efficient.

The rain is a fine drizzle, warm on the skin as I head northwest and then west to pass between the Babsons and the Torrey Islands and northwest again out in the reach. There is not much wind, just a light zephyr from the southeast. There isn't much traffic, either, just a few lobster boats plying their trade in a monotone world, gray water, gray shore, gray sky . . .

I hear the muffled putter of a marine engine behind me and look aft to see a wooden ketch coming up from astern. It seems as though two out of every three boats I am seeing on this cruise are wooden ketches. How many can there be?

As this one draws abreast of us I recognize the old boy who asked about *Penelope*'s boom. He is accompanied by a crew of three or four winsome young women in their twenties. How does he do it? I wonder. He is clearly at least as old as I am, a grizzled old dog pushing seventy, just like me. Maybe they are his daughters or perhaps a class of novice sailors. Well, I certainly hope so.

They wave prettily and go chugging off into the distance. About now we are passing Center Harbor, which surely must rank as the wooden boat capital of the world. Packed into this small anchorage are more beautiful wooden sailing craft than you are ever likely to see anywhere else (the one exception being the wooden boat regatta that starts and finishes once a year from WoodenBoat next door).

The anchorage at Center Harbor lies off the Brooklin Boatyard run by Steve White, grandson of author and *New Yorker* fixture E. B. White. The yard is as wonderful as the harbor, with shed after shed full of classic boats and yachts. The easier ways of an earlier time live on here, and a discreet visitor can wander unchallenged through the sheds and take it all in.

E. B. White himself was a lifelong sailor who lived for many years on a farm in Brooklin. His essay "The Sea and the Wind That Blows" may well be the best short piece ever written on why we sail. Find and read it if you can.

We ghost on past Center Harbor and soon find ourselves off the Benjamin River. This is an almost perfectly landlocked harbor, also full of classic wooden boats. One that I used to visit every year was the C. C. Hanley cat ketch *Mollie B*, which Maynard Bray kept here until recently. Another favorite is the handsome Chinese-red twenty-five-foot Folkboat *Tomahawk*, which was sailed to Cuba and back a few years ago. Then there is the majestic gaff sloop *Vela*, sleek and shapely in her smooth coat of black paint. Less interesting to me but certainly awesome in her way is a plus-or-minus forty-footer aptly named *Yar*. All perfect brightwork and polished bronze, she is so immaculate that it is hard to imagine anyone actually taking her out and sailing her.

Back on the reach the breeze is picking up a little, and we are encountering the first of a batch of large sloops engaged in some kind of race that seems to cover a considerable distance. They appear as

tiny specks to the northwest and will disappear the same way to the southeast. We do our best to give them all the right-of-way and are interested to note the various attitudes of the different crews. Some are all grim business and refuse to even look at us as they pass. Others wave. Some offer compliments. Sadly, the friendliest of all, the one brimming with politesse and goodwill, is also the one struggling along in last place.

All the racers behind us now, we near the Deer Isle Bridge. This is an impressive structure that seems way out of place in its surroundings. The architecture and infrastructure in these parts are human in scale, reflecting the rural nature of the area. Coming upon a giant mile-long suspension bridge here is something like encountering a spaceship from another planet.

Today the bridge is crawling with workers, part of the nationwide repair and upgrading program that began when an unseemly number of these structures began collapsing due to advanced age and neglect. As I sail under the bridge, the roar of jackhammers and rivet guns rings in my ears, mixing with the crashing and clanking of heavy machinery. I flinch involuntarily, fearing a large hunk of something may hurtle down on us from so high overhead, bringing an abrupt and definitive end to our cruise. It would make for an ironic kind of sailing accident.

Penelope escapes unscathed, and we continue in the direction of Bucks Harbor. Some kids in an open twenty-three- or twenty-four-foot day sailer pass us going the other way then immediately do a 180-degree turn so that they are running along behind us about fifty yards back. It looks like they have decided to have a little fun showing up the old gaffer. Or maybe they have just decided it is time to go home. In any case, if they thought they could catch *Penelope*, they were mistaken. Soon they and their boat are only a insignificant speck in the distance.

Warm though the persistent drizzle is, I am beginning to feel chilled after a few not very active hours out in the cockpit. I contemplate heading into Bucks Harbor for the night, but a look at the forest of masts in there is somehow intimidating. I'm feeling a little tired as well as cold, and for once the idea of anchoring under sail in a really crowded place is just too daunting to face.

Orcutt Harbor, a long narrow gut running southwest–northeast with Cape Rosier to the west and a peninsula tipped by Condon

Point to the east, is just a few more miles along my route and—this is what I like about it today—is described in Taft and Rindlaub (the Maine coast cruiser's bible) as "little used by yachtsmen."

Penelope reaches all the way up into the gut, just over one nautical mile, and I note that if the wind is onshore next day, we will have a longish beat all the way out of there with the breeze right on our nose. We anchor right at the head of the harbor, not far from a Bristol-fashion fifty-foot sloop on a mooring, the only other boat anywhere near.

Except for five or six yachts moored in a little indentation along the eastern shore about half a mile away, there are no other boats at all. Bucks Harbor crammed full like a sardine can only a few miles away, and this place with only a lone visitor—me . . . it says something about the herd instinct in man. I'm not sure what, exactly, but I'm glad that it is so.

I quickly realize that, among its other attractions, Orcutt Harbor is home to an astonishing number of ospreys. In my experience, ospreys usually operate in pairs with a centrally located nest and a territory to themselves. But here there are five or six pairs all wheeling around overhead and stooping on what seems to be an inexhaustible supply of fish.

Osprey nests can be quite monumental and are frequently passed down through the generations. There are several on the Maine coast said to have been in continuous occupancy for a hundred years or more. The nest on Pulpit Rock outside Pulpit Harbor is one, and there is another not too far away on a ledge off Oak Hill at the northeast tip of North Haven Island that is so big, it could almost be a fortress built for men, not birds. Here at Orcutt Harbor there are any number of birds, but I don't see any nests, so perhaps what I'm seeing is a special avian convention.

I am having a wonderful time watching the wheeling, screeching, diving birds, but I am also learning that, along with ospreys, Orcutt Harbor is home to an impressive population of mosquitoes. The wet weather we have enjoyed all summer has upped the mosquito count everywhere. In fact it has been so bad that the time-honored tradition of "mosquito hour" is no longer in effect.

In normal years, when the mosquitoes arrived at an anchorage around sunset you could button up your boat for an hour or so, then open her up again confident that mosquito hour was over. Not this year. There are mosquitoes before mosquito hour and mosquitoes after it. In fact there are sometimes mosquitoes in the middle of the day in the middle of large areas of water, far from land . . . But here in Orcutt Harbor it is even worse than elsewhere. Reluctantly, I retreat below and pull the companionway hatch and doors shut behind me.

Leaving the boat open for so long was a big mistake. The cabin is already full of mosquitoes and I am not well equipped to deal with them. For reasons having to do with my reluctance to spend time in a small enclosed space full of poison, I don't carry and won't use insecticides. Thus, my only way of dealing with mosquitoes is to hunt them down one by one, a not very efficient endeavor. Alternatively, I can take to my sleeping bag, pull the covers over my head, and cower there, still being bitten by the considerable number of enterprising creatures that manage to get inside with me. This is not a good option now because I haven't cooked and eaten yet, and I have a real day-on-the-water, fresh-air-type appetite going.

Reluctantly, and despite a deep-seated mistrust of chemical companies (the people who brought us DDT and Agent Orange, after all), I do carry Deep Woods Off or other DEET formulations and, in extremis, use them. My current situation qualifies and I proceed to douse myself with the stuff. An uneasy chemical truce established between myself and my winged tormentors, I can cook, eat, drink, and make an early night of it.

Tuesday, August 12, I wake up early to the sound of torrential rain pouring down and crashing on the cabin top. It is a little like being inside a snare drum but I like it, really. It reminds me of when I was a kid and slept in a room with a tin roof overhead.

It is about 6 a.m. and there isn't much point in getting up yet. Nothing to do outside but get drenched and not much to do inside, either, but read or listen to the radio. I flick on the weather radio and hear news of record rainfalls moving up the coast. This is going to be the kind of day when your dinghy fills right up to the gunwales and floats only because of the air compartments at bow and stern. I switch to Maine Public Radio and drift off again listening to the world and local news being repeated over and over again as it always is at this time of day.

By eight o'clock I am awake again and restless. I can't sleep all day although it would be good if I could. The rain is still pouring down undiminished and, peering out one of the port lights, I can't see anything but sheets of water. I pull one of the large wine jugs I use for drinking water out of the bilge and measure out a mugful into my all-purpose stainless pot for coffee. Beans go into my German hand grinder from the Lehman's catalog (old-fashioned stuff for Mennonites and other throwbacks like myself) and grind away happily. Not only will my coffee be better than something out of a can or jar, but I am thankful for these small, pleasant tasks. It promises to be a long day.

The coffee is good. Colombian Supremo twice as strong as recommended, and twice as much of it in my special mug as you would get in a regular cup. Suddenly, inexplicably, I am very happy. It is good to be here in my diminutive boat with the rain pouring down. Good food, good books . . . we really have everything we need. I find that I am looking forward to the day after all.

The day does pass quite pleasantly. There were a couple of short breaks in the weather when I was able to get a little exercise in the dinghy and, for the rest, the books from WoodenBoat and my CD player provided ample entertainment. It was cozy and snug aboard as we whiled away the hours in a kind of warm, damp funk.

Because of the rain and the ever-present mosquitoes, I had to keep *Penelope* buttoned right up for most of the time, leaving the interior a little dark and cheerless. To combat this I fired up a large hurricane lamp as well as the gimbaled kerosene lamp on the main bulkhead. This took care of the cheer department very nicely and provided some warmth, but around nightfall I noticed that droplets of water had started falling from various points on the cabin roof. For a brief moment I wondered if it had rained so hard that rain had found its way right through the solid cabin top, but investigation revealed that the inside of the entire hull and deck was filmed with water. Since it is well known that solid fuel makes for a dry boat whereas oil stoves make for a wet one, I deduced that the problem was condensation caused by burning the oil lamps in so much humidity. I quickly doused the lamps before all that water started running off into my bedding, books, and supplies.

Lying in the dark I listened to quirky riffs, off rhythms, and discords from the inimitable Thelonious Monk blending with the still-thunderous rain beating down on deck until I fell into a pleasant, dreamless sleep. Another early evening aboard *Penelope*.

14. Things That Come in the Night

The engineless sailboat can't always go where she wants to. It is a corollary of this that she cannot always get out of places she would like to leave.

Frequently heavy weather is preceded by a couple of days of calm. The engineless boat that is lying in a poorly protected anchorage may know something bad is on its way but, lacking wind, may not be able to do anything to avoid it. For this reason, among others, serious ground tackle and the know-how to deploy it are mandatory for the engineless sailor.

It is also true that very bad weather can arrive unannounced, and, despite all the best efforts of the meteorologists at NOAA, it frequently does. Sailors of all kinds, motorless and otherwise, should keep this in mind and always adjust their anchoring practice accordingly.

An afternoon in late July last year found me in the popular and well-regarded anchorage between McGlathery and Round Islands, which form part of Merchants Row, south of Deer Isle, Maine.

I had been suffering through a week of unusually light and variable winds, and, in fact, had been unable to continue homeward toward Swan's Island for the past two days. Certain essential supplies

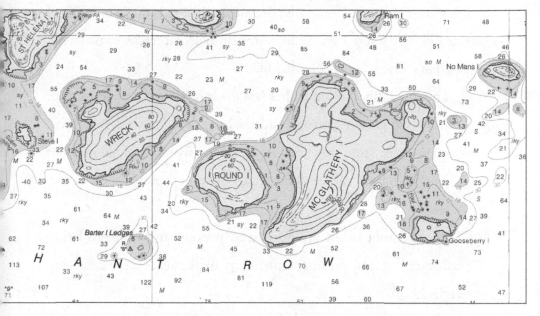

like beer were running low and I had read all the books on board.

My mood had not been improved by daylong battles with the nasty small flies that always show up in this kind of weather to bite your ankles and generally make life miserable. In short I'd developed a serious case of the nautical version of cabin fever.

Well, at least the nights were calm tranquil and undisturbed. I enjoyed a rather undistinguished dinner (supplies in that department were running low, too) and went to bed.

Lying in my bunk with the hatch open it was pleasant to watch a spectacular array of stars wheel overhead until sleep came.

Somewhere around 2 a.m. I was awakened by a strange noise. It sounded like there was a freight train off in the distance, running fast, and coming my way.

Closer and closer it came and louder and louder its rushing roaring sound became. Could I be dreaming this? A little disoriented, I was still pretty sure I wasn't anchored on railroad tracks somewhere, but that's sure what it sounded like.

The squall hit and suddenly I was the inhabitant of a paint mixer. *Penelope* was standing on end and crashing down in wild, mean seas that had come from nowhere. At times she would veer sideways to the onslaught and roll until her high cockpit combings were nearly under.

I could only lie in my bunk and prevent myself from being thrown out of it by pushing with all my might against the cabin top overhead.

This went on for fifteen minutes, and then stopped as quickly and decisively as it had begun.

I was thankful that the anchor I had down was oversized for my boat, and connected to its rode by fifteen feet of chain so heavy that it frequently elicits comments from other sailors when they see it lying along my deck. Thankful also that, in addition to the anchor and the extra-heavy chain, I had deployed a twenty-five-pound sentinel, a lead pig that rides about a third of the way down my anchor rode and relieves strain on the anchor by forming a catenary.

All this heavy gear was no doubt excessive for a calm night at the end of an entire week of calms. But without it, that brief maelstrom, which was the wildest fifteen minutes I have ever spent on any boat in sixty-some years of sailing, would surely have sent us up on the unyielding granite of the McGlathery Island shore.

Next day was as airless and enervating as all those that had preceded it. Fly swatter in hand, seething at the injustice of it all, I
passed another unhappy day. Hot, frustrated, fly-bitten, bored.

At around four in the afternoon a hopeful little breeze sprang up.
Normally, I would have ignored such an unassuming latecomer. The
engineless sailor prefers an earlier departure and some assurance that
a breeze will last, but I was hot to get out of there.

Up went the sail, and up came the anchor, and we began ghosting
eastward along the McGlathery shore. No sooner did we near the
eastern anchorage at McGlathery than my promising little breeze
forgot its promise altogether and betrayed me totally. We lay drifting
aimlessly on a mirror-like sea.

I rowed into the closest part of the anchorage, a little bowl-like
depression in the southwest corner. The bowl is formed by a steep,
smooth rock shore that rises to the beginning of vegetation about
thirty feet above the water. It's a snug little spot with the shore rising
amphitheater-like on three sides.

Weather for the night ahead was forecast as light and variable becoming five knots from the southwest. It looked like I was in a fine
spot—the most perfectly sheltered in the anchorage—so I dropped
the hook then and there, unconcerned that, contrary to my usual
practice, I was anchored quite close to shore.

Soon enough the breeze came, not out of the southwest as predicted but from the northeast with a vast stretch of water to windward.
And not at five knots, but at ten, then fifteen, then twenty-five. Now

I found myself pinned in my snug little amphitheater and to my consternation, I noted that the growing waves were crashing on a rocky shore only around twenty yards behind my rudder.

By ten o'clock that evening the wind had risen to an estimated thirty to thirty-five knots, accompanied by driving rain and heavy seas. This was a repeat of the paint-mixer experience, only now I was on a lee shore with rocks almost at spitting distance astern.

I had my same heavy ground tackle down, and now I could only hope that it would hold. It was far too rough to try to row another anchor out, and deploying one from the boat would be useless because, if we dragged, it would have no chance to set before we hit the rocks. The big fisherman-type anchors that I carry for just such emergencies weren't going to help me here.

I thought about my situation and realized that if we went up, it would be more than the boat I lost. The slimy surface and slope of the little amphitheater behind me were such that I would have no chance to climb up to safety.

It seemed somehow unfair that this popular anchorage, a place for lighthearted summer adventures, could suddenly become a life-threatening trap.

It blew all night, and once again I spent most of it pushing against the cabin roof to keep from being thrown out of my bunk. Lying in the bunk was somehow preferable to watching the seas breaking on the nearby shore and wondering when we would join them. I resolved then and there that, if I got out of this, I would never again, under any circumstances, anchor close to shore.

In the morning the wind moderated and changed direction. Now I had a breeze that would get me home, and I was very happy to take advantage of it.

15. The Mysterious Samaritan

I had started off earlier in the day from Swan's Island bound for the Cranberry Islands but after passing between Black and Placentia Islands and getting to a point near the Bass Harbor Bar, the wind fell light. I decided to postpone the open-ocean portion of my route because the possibility of spending the night becalmed off Long Ledge and the Western Way was not inviting.

Thus it was that I steered to port and headed for Bass Harbor, which—somewhat exposed and always uneasy due to heavy lobster boat traffic—was the only alternative. Only partway there, the breeze quit altogether and we lay, motionless except for a slight bobble, contemplating the moored boats along shore and wishing we could join them.

As time passed, I was confident some little evening zephyr would spring up. They almost always do, especially when the tide changes. But I was growing impatient because it is always best to anchor early and cook dinner before the mosquitoes arrive and you have to batten down the hatches.

Off in the distance I began to hear an unfamiliar noise: *poka poka poka, pop pop pop, poka poka*, a series of muffled explosions as though someone was firing off a child's popgun rapidly and over and over.

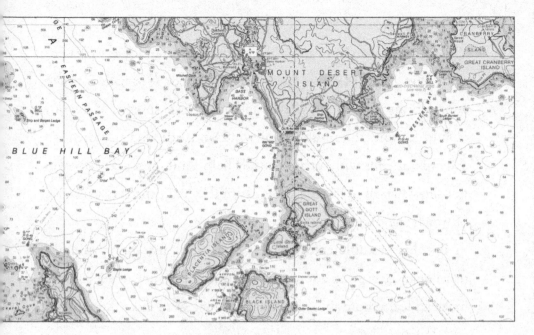

Clearly mechanical, this sound, unlike the whine and roar of modern engines, was not at all unpleasant. It did not overpower or obliterate natural sounds (the lapping of wavelets, the cry of seabirds) but joined them in a companionable way.

Off to the south a speck emerged from some low-lying mist and grew slowly until it revealed itself as a low graceful launch approaching at a modest four or five knots. This boat was in the water the way a sea duck or a seal is, not on it or above it, or even against it, as the modern mechanical monstrosities that call themselves boats these days seem to be.

Clearly, although this was a powerboat, a man aboard her was still a part of his environment; he could feel the movement of the sea as a smooth, silky surge, not a series of jarring collisions, and like a sailor in an easy breeze, he would have the time and the inclination for philosophy.

This apparition from an earlier day drew close and a very pleasant gentleman asked if I would like a tow into harbor. Normally *Penelope* considers any idea of a tow as an indignity. Our sport is to use our wits to fathom the mysteries of wind and tide and use them to achieve our ends without any outside help. And more, *Penelope* will not allow herself to be seen being assisted by craft the very existence of which she disapproves.

But this was different. Here was a beautiful, intriguing, and unusual boat. Accepting a tow would allow us a chance to get a better look and learn more about her. Besides, there were those mosquitoes, and dinner.

"I wouldn't say no," I said and tossed a line over to the boat, which was named *Goslin*. Before we got under way I got a look under her engine hatch at the antique Acadia one-lunger, which bore a striking resemblance to the old piston water pumps we had on our Long Island wells when I was a boy (they, too, were quieter and pleasanter than what came after).

Goslin and *Penelope* then chugged pleasantly into the harbor. My benefactor dropped me off over a good anchoring spot and departed as he had come: *poka poka poka, pop pop, poka poka* . . . into the mist.

I tried to take a picture of *Goslin* as she departed, but, oddly, when I downloaded that day's images into my laptop, the frame that should have depicted *Goslin* showed only mist and an empty expanse of water.

16. What's for Dinner?:
A Single-Hander's Galley Strategies

Theories abound as to why some sailors choose to go it alone, eschewing the warmth of human company as they venture forth on the waters. Serious misanthropy is often suspected, or a simple lack of friends or mates, but more often than not I think it is really only the desire for complete freedom.

This quest for freedom usually includes a desire to be as free as possible from the recurring drudgery of daily tasks like cooking and cleaning up afterward. Our single-hander is willing to do the necessary to eat reasonably well, but strives to keep the whole process simple. He would rather have a glass of wine after dinner than do the dishes. Managing this can become a sport and a pastime in itself.

Let's start with provisioning. While almost anything tastes good after a strenuous day on the water, fresh or frozen foods are definitely preferable to the stuff that comes in cans or plastic boxes. An efficient system is required to provide a steady supply of these better victuals on a regular basis.

Let's say that we are going for a cruise among the islands of the Maine coast for a week or so. We are not going to visit towns or stores, so if we want to avoid a diet of corned beef hash and baked beans, a small but acceptable amount of planning and preparation are necessary.

At the heart of our strategy will be a large cooler of the type advertised to keep ice for five days in ninety-five-degree weather. This claim may be exaggerated, but, properly managed, these coolers will definitely keep ice for considerably more than five days when located out of the sun and somewhere near the cool bilges of a boat in New England waters.

First to enter our cooler will be the ice, two or three gallon plastic jugs nearly full of frozen water (allow some room for expansion). Ice made in jugs will not flood the cooler as it melts, and the continued presence of very cold water around the remaining ice inhibits the thawing process. Next on this lowest level will be the frozen ingredients for a meal planned for the last day of our voyage—half a bag of frozen peas, let's say, and some frozen, boiled potatoes ready to make home fries when thawed, and a couple of nice frozen fillets of haddock.

Next comes a layer, many sheets thick, of newspaper. This protective layer will not be disturbed again until it is time to prepare that meal. Frozen ingredients for each preceding meal are then layered above the first, each separated by an insulating layer of newspaper. The coldest layer will be down at the bottom with the ice, and as we go upward each layer will be just a little less cold. Thus the highest layer (first meal) will thaw first, becoming ready to cook, and so on as we uncover new layers each day, much in the manner of an archaeological dig.

In contrast, a randomly stocked cooler will not function adequately because the contents will be continually exposed to warm air while one rummages for desired items with the lid open. It is important, by the way, to keep the cooler mostly full, so add more newspaper, sail bags, or even some of the less offensive items from your laundry as successive layers come out.

Using our system it may actually occur that things do not thaw fast enough! So check your upcoming evening's meal each morning and transfer it to the bilge if it is still frozen hard. There it will gently thaw by dinnertime.

Not everything we eat need come from the cooler. Bags of fresh spinach, for example, will last quite well if simply kept in the bilge. Ditto for onions, tomatoes, eggs, butter, mayonnaise, mustard, and so forth. Bread, pasta, and donuts will keep well almost anywhere.

We have not mentioned, but also use food items that can be obtained from our surroundings. Fish, particularly mackerel, are often easy to catch, and mussels are frequently available for the taking (be sure to check for any red tide alerts in your area). Most lobstermen are willing to sell some of their catch right off the boat, frequently at wholesale prices.

Whenever I go by the oyster farm along one of my cruising routes, I add a sack full of those ambrosial mollusks to my larder. I keep a clam hoe on board, too, but sadly opportunities to use it are ever fewer. Clamming in Maine has always been an occupation of last resort. Anyone who was down and out could always head for the clam flats and make a few bucks. As development, overuse, and pollution have reduced the number of good clamming areas, pressure on those remaining areas has become overwhelming and unsustainable. We see it on Swan's Island (sometimes known as "Clam Island"), where the clamming is still fairly good. If local law enforcement spent the time necessary to keep clam pirates from other locales off the flats, they wouldn't be able to do anything else.

Ready to start cooking now, and here's where the art of simplification really comes in. Let's say we are going to have a meal of steak, pasta, and fresh spinach. How do we keep quality high and work to a minimum from start to finish?

Take a large stainless pot two-thirds full of seawater, bring to a boil, and add a fistful of angel hair (cooks faster than regular spaghetti, saves fuel). When the pasta is half done add fresh spinach to the pot. When the pasta is done the spinach will be also. (When discussing such economies the early-twentieth-century British boating writer F. B. Cooke mentioned making coffee from water that had just been used to boil eggs, but I'm inclined to think you have to draw the line somewhere.)

Drain the cooked contents of the pot into a colander held overside then add them to the frying pan in which your steak has been frying in olive oil on the other burner. Swirl the pasta and spinach in the meat juices and oil, and season to taste (you won't need salt). Eat from the frying pan. The pot is already clean and ready to heat water for coffee in the morning, and the frying pan and utensils will be easy to wipe off with paper towels after they have soaked in seawater overnight.

If you want bread or something else along with the meal, use of a plastic-coated paper plate is permissible. I had one paper plate, used in this auxiliary capacity, that lasted for three years of extensive cruising. I only had to part with it after I made the mistake of slicing onions on it. The knife blade penetrated the plastic, and mold eventually got into those cuts. I had become quite fond of my plate and enjoyed speculating on how far into the future we could go together (an item for the *Guinness Book of Records*?), so I was really sorry to say good-bye.

Breakfast will be black coffee and blueberry donuts or a mouthwatering kind of semisweet oatmeal cookie that my wife knows how to make, and lunch might be skinless and boneless sardines on bread with mayonnaise and sliced tomatoes (the paper plate comes in here).

Finally, it should be noted that while fresher foods are always preferred, no well-found vessel leaves her mooring without a backup supply of certain old favorites of the canned or, possibly, the freeze-dried variety. Dinty Moore, Chef Boyardee, and others can all step in and provide an acceptable or even a memorable meal on occasion, and Newman's Own mango salsa has added zest to many a seaborne repast. Someday I may write about the wonders of the Spamburger with Vermont cheddar cheese, Vidalia onion, and Louisiana hot sauce, but that is another story.

17. Bad Night at the Barred Islands

This goes back to my early days with *Penelope*. She still had a motor then, but not the two big fisherman anchors she carries now.

Taft and Rindlaub's useful *Cruising Guide to the Maine Coast* has this to say about the anchorage at the Barred Islands in Penobscot Bay: "You will be comfortable here in settled summer weather, but the anchorage can be rough and untenable in strong winds from the southwest, north or northwest, especially at high tide when the bars are covered. If these conditions are expected, leave."

I guess my first mistake was that, although the weather seemed settled on that day quite a few years ago, it was no longer summer, but getting on into late November. Along this coast, *November* and *settled weather* are expressions that don't always fit comfortably in the same sentence.

NOAA had predicted a week or so of bluebird weather, a kind of late-season Indian summer with moderate winds and unseasonably warm weather. Anxious to take advantage of this unexpected gift, I decided to squeeze in a short cruise before the inevitable late-season trip to the marine railway in Bass Harbor for hauling and storage.

It was the work of a morning to throw together some foodstuffs and ferry them out to *Penelope* at her mooring. Then Truffle, my

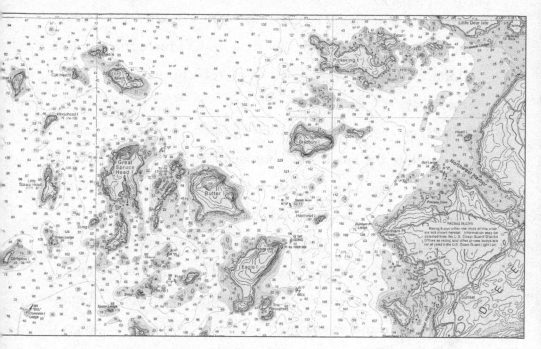

large and frequently boisterous Chesapeake Bay retriever, and I were ready to go. We slipped the mooring and reached out of the harbor in a moderate northwest breeze, bound west.

As frequently happens, what was a moderate northwest breeze in the harbor was considerably more than moderate outside. For some reason, moderate southwest breezes in the harbor often turn out to be feeble or nonexistent when you get out into Toothacher Bay, but the nor'westers wear sheep's clothing in harbor, and frequently show wolf after you round Hockamock Head and reach the bay.

We needed a reef right away, and I tied it in while Truffle frolicked on deck, snapping at loose lines and giving me the occasional affectionate nip. Thus assisted, the job was quickly done.

Off Merchants Row, we faced the usual decision as to whether to push on across East Penobscot Bay or pick a convenient anchorage and leave further progress for tomorrow. Certainly there was no shortage of wind, so we opted to go for Vinalhaven, across the smoky bay.

Soon enough we were off Bluff Head on Vinalhaven, a mile or two south of the Fox Island Thoroughfare. Bluff Head marks the opening to deep, fjord-like Winter Harbor, and also the way to Seal Bay, an enchantingly lovely body of water just inside Hen Island.

There are (or were then) few habitations around Seal Bay, and although in summer a few cruisers might find their way in, on this November night it would be all mine, a late-season bonus. Rounding Little Hen and proceeding a short way to the east, we dropped the hook in about ten feet at low water.

I rowed Truffle to a small island west of the anchorage where once a summer cottage had stood, marked now only by the charred but still-standing chimney and fireplace. While Truffle attended to business, I was amused to note that a whiskey bottle I had placed on the mantel a couple of years before, souvenir of a memorable picnic, was still there.

Truff and I returned to *Penelope*, where we enjoyed a hearty dinner. The whirring wings of flights of sea ducks made a strange and haunting music in the quiet of the evening, and Truff and I were lulled to sleep by it, along with the cries of Canada geese and the odd tootling of oldsquaw.

Morning dawned clear and, for the time of year, pleasantly warm.

The wind was onshore, southwest now—just right for progress up the bay. Truffle and I had a leisurely breakfast, then went for a long row in the warm, golden sun. As on the night before, sea ducks were all around in great profusion.

They begin to appear in late October, migrating south from their summer haunts in the Arctic. By mid-November they have transformed the Maine coast, the sounds and sight of them everywhere. Big rafts of eiders and scoters, swift flights of oldsquaw, lively, playful, splashing flotillas of buffleheads.

Truffle was clearly puzzled and a little disgruntled that we were not hunting all these abundant birds, but more and more as I get older, I prefer to just watch and listen.

We hauled anchor at the leisurely hour of eleven and reached out into East Penobscot Bay. Now we hung a left at the entrance to the Fox Island Thoroughfare, alternately reaching and beating along that seven-mile stretch that separates Vinalhaven and North Haven, and provides a passage from East to West Penobscot Bay.

In summer the thoroughfare is a busy place with an endless stream of boats and yachts going east and west, but now it was almost deserted. There were a few workboats to be seen and a few yachts moored off the old-fashioned and thoroughly wonderful J. O. Brown's Boatyard, waiting for a late-season haul-out.

Arriving at Stand Off Point, at the west end of the thoroughfare, we steer to starboard and begin reaching northwesterly down the north side of North Haven Island. Off Pulpit Harbor we wonder if it is time to call it a day, but there is plenty of daylight left and a good breeze. We decide to try for some locale a little wilder and more remote for this evening.

Northward we scud in a perfect full-sail breeze. *Penelope* is eating up the miles, a boiling, alabaster bone in her teeth. *Argos*, the dinghy, follows, riding high on a cushion of foam. Late afternoon finds us in the neighborhood of Butter Island, and with dusk approaching we nip into the quiet and solitude of the Barred Island anchorage.

The Barred Islands, which include Big Barred to the east, Little Barred to the west, and Escargot and Bartender to the north, are a grouping of uncommon beauty. Nature has shaped the tidal bars surrounding them with all the grace and delicacy of a Japanese garden. At low tide, they are a wonder to behold.

To the south, a gravel bar connects Big and Little Barred, and although it just barely shows at low water, its presence is what protects the anchorage from the southwest. Since NOAA is predicting only a modest southwest breeze for the night, I snuggle up to this bar and anchor close under its lee.

This evening is even milder than the preceding one so Truff and I while away a pleasant time in the cockpit, enjoying dinner and, in my case, the better part of a bottle of very nice Côtes du Rhône. Then it's off to bed, and pleasant dreams while *Penelope* rocks gently in the near calm.

WHAM! BANG!—A brutal crashing noise, a violent lurch, and *Penelope* is canted over and suddenly inert, no longer cradled by the sea. I become aware of a howling, rushing, roaring tumult of sound.

Groggily I feel for the companionway hatch, slide it back, and flinch at the sudden lashing of the icy rain-filled wind. Looking forward, I can barely make out the bowsprit in the horizontal driving rain. Looking aft I can make out ugly half-submerged rocks close astern.

I point a flashlight straight down at the water, seeing rocky bottom only a few feet below the surface. Nothing is visible more than ten feet from the boat. I have no idea where we are. Most likely we are aground somewhere in the anchorage but since I didn't wake up when we started to drag anchor, but only when we struck unyielding rock, nothing is certain. We could be anywhere.

Glancing at my watch, I see that it is now about an hour before dead low tide. Clearly I will have to take some action if I don't want to get pushed farther up onto the rocks when the tide comes in. I think it may be possible, if just barely, to row an anchor out into deeper water. With an anchor out, we can hope that *Penelope* will float free and hold her position as the tide rises.

Hauling the dinghy even with the cockpit I lower our second anchor, a twenty-five-pound CQR, into the dinghy just aft of the central thwart. It would be better to have a big fisherman-type anchor for duty on this rocky bottom, but such was not yet part of our equipment. (*Penelope* now carries two of them, along with the twenty- and twenty-five-pound CQRs.)

On top of the CQR and its chain I coil 150 feet of nylon rode, the bottom of the coil attached to the anchor chain and the top, or bitter, end attached to the mooring cleat up forward on *Penelope*. Thus, as I row away from *Penelope*, line will feed from the dinghy, causing little resistance as we progress.

Even with this precaution, the row away from the mother ship is perilously difficult. Enough sea comes over the rail of the dinghy that water in the bilge soon sloshes well above my ankles.

We proceed in fits and starts, frequently blown backward in the gusts or forced back by an extra-large wave. It all comes down to a matter of whether we can get the anchor out far enough before the dinghy is swamped.

We just make it, taking an extra-large dollop of green water aboard as we tip the anchor over the transom.

It is worth noting that we only succeeded here because we had a proper old-fashioned rowing rig with solid bronze oarlocks, properly sized oars, and a good boat. If we had the stubby oars and shallow potmetal oarlocks you see everywhere today, it could not have been done. If we had been towing an inflatable instead of a rigid dinghy, well, fuggedaboudit, as Tony Soprano used to say.

Now we were blown back skittering wildly over the swells to *Penelope* with bilgewater reaching halfway up my calves. Nothing to do now but wait for the tide to turn, and see if the new anchor would hold.

Soaked and shivering, I huddled in the cabin with Truff and drank hot coffee until, after what seemed like a very long time, *Pene-*

lope began to stir on the rising tide. With mercifully little pounding, she floated free and rode to the kedge.

I couldn't rest easy, though. There was the question as to whether the kedge would continue to hold on that rocky bottom. Our situation had improved greatly, but clearly we would be better off in deeper water, and back over mud.

Shore had to be to the east of us. I still couldn't see it in the driving rain and, now, fog, but I could hear surf in that direction. So it seemed that an attempt to go west, away from the nearby rocks and the shore, made sense.

As mentioned earlier, *Penelope* still had an engine in those days and, although I hadn't run it in a month, now seemed like a good time to try. Unexpectedly and surely undeservedly the Universal Diesel started right up.

Motors on my boats, when I've had them at all, have always been maligned, mistreated, and mistrusted creatures, resented for their demands, and cursed for their problems and failures, but this one, in this moment, came to know the fullness of my love.

Leaving the trusty, the noble and heroic iron wind to warm up, I went forward, buoyed anchor number one, and cast it off. Then, proceeding at dead slow, I was able to run up on the kedge, retrieve it, and we were off!

Blind, but, happy and hopeful, we ran west for open water.

WHAM!—A terrific shock as we run head-on into another rock. I'm thrown forward against the binnacle, and *Penelope* glances off on a crazy tangent. I dive for the controls and cut the engine. We float in the fog, rain, and encompassing darkness. Anchor down again, we decide to wait for first light, which now is not too far off. No more adventures into the inscrutable unknown.

With dawn the rain stopped, the wind died, and the fog dissipated. Shapes emerged out of the gloom, and I learned that we had gone up on the west side of the anchorage, not the eastern one, as I had thought.

I still don't know why I had heard surf to the east but not to the west. In any case, running west on the motor was a serious mistake, for which we could have paid much more dearly than we did.

In daylight, I retrieved our first anchor, found a nice spot in the middle of the anchorage, put both anchors down with all the scope available, and slept for the remainder of the day, and all the next night.

The rest of our late-autumnal excursion was blessedly uneventful. We headed home via the Eggemoggin Reach, got there, and were happy enough to call the boating season over for that year.

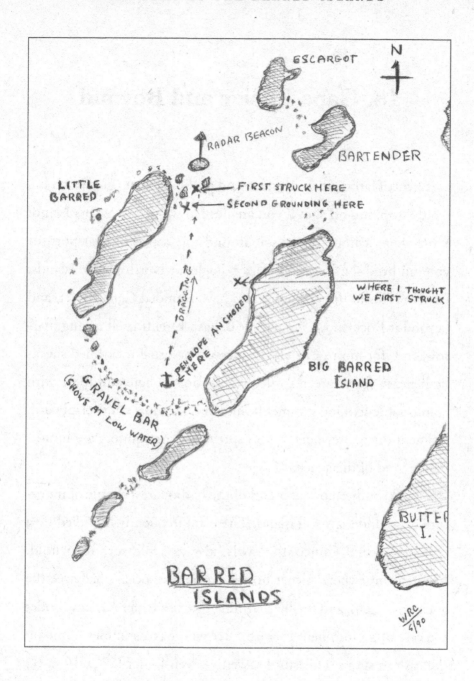

18. Cape Rosier and Beyond

Orcutt Harbor at the western end of the Eggemoggin Reach is a handy stopping-off spot if you are headed west from Swan's Island. From there it is a pleasant sail around to Castine or Searsport, or you can head south toward Butter, Eagle, or North Haven Islands. Islesboro lies to the west once you have rounded Cape Rosier, and beyond it Rockland, Camden, or Belfast. Orcutt itself is long, narrow, and, for most of its length, deep. The usual rock-lined shores lie beneath forest-green spruce woods dotted here and there with comfortable-looking summer homes of traditional white clapboard. As mentioned elsewhere, both ospreys and mosquitoes are inordinately fond of this place.

At the southern or outer end of the harbor are a couple of moorings close under a small island. These are frequently occupied by a pair of graceful Concordia Yawls, always a pleasure to behold. Moored somewhere farther up the harbor, we occasionally see the ancient, famous, and totally charming Swedish gaffer *Elly* now under the care of a prominent yacht broker who has a summer home on the eastern shore. This sturdy twenty-seven-footer (27' x 10' x 6') once fished for a living in Scandinavian waters somewhere around 140 years ago. In those days, a popular way to store your boat for the winter was to sink it over a soft mud bottom, and bring it up again in the spring. Thus the boat was spared the expansion and contraction caused by drying out, and also tended to be pickled inside and out by good salt brine. Such early treatment may have had something to do with *Elly*'s impressive longevity.

Converted for pleasure sailing and said by many to be the oldest yacht in America still in commission, she has had a long career under the stewardship of a family in the Martin River area of Nova Scotia. The talented marine artist Bill Gilkerson qualified by marriage, and his very moving accounts of sailing and caring for the old girl can be found in the archives of *WoodenBoat* magazine. At last hearing *Elly* had come south to seek a new home, age (of her owners) and health problems forcing her reluctant sale.

Wednesday, Orcutt Harbor

There is no wind as yet so I laze around on deck with coffee and a book. I'm reading a collection of Lincoln Colcord's stories. Descendant of a long line of Searsport sea captains, Colcord grew up on sailing ships in the China trade, but came up just too late to become a mariner in sail himself so turned to journalism and fiction. His tales of monsoons, piracy, shipwreck, and wily, pigtailed Chinamen bear the stylistic stamp of another era, but are worth more than a look nonetheless. My great hero Sterling Hayden, author and topmast man on the *Gertrude M. Thebault* among other accomplishments, was a friend and great fan of his, so how could I be otherwise?

It's hot in the cockpit and I am slowly baking. Just when I think I will have to take a swim or indulge in some other form of basting, a nice little breeze springs up, providentially out of the northwest. We will not have to tack all the way out of this narrow mile-long gut after all, not that doing so would be any terrible ordeal. Particularly since she shed her propeller, *Penelope* is very close-winded and easy to sail to weather. No sheets to bother with, and she never misses stays.

But reaching is easier still, and it is fine to be ghosting silently along in the morning sun, quiet and serene as a milkweed seed floating on the August breeze. We clear Orcutt Harbor and make our way along the Cape Rosier shore. Here we encounter a haunting vision from another era. A Mower-designed Sea Bird yawl is ghosting along piloted by a bearded old salt who seems very appropriate to his ancient craft. She has a grace and simplicity seldom encountered today and looks like she belongs in her element in a way few modern boats can emulate.

We are headed southwest at what seems to be a safe distance from shore and approaching a point off the mouth of Horseshoe Cove (another deep gut into the cape) when I happen to look overside and see rock bottom only a few feet down. Noting that it is all too easy to become relaxed and stupid while enjoying a sunny summer morning, I quickly swing the wheel to port, steering for more sea room and deep water.

A little farther on we pass a five-foot spot shown on the chart as "Barney's Mistake." Poor Barney. I wonder what the full story of his adventure was. Did he, too, become overly relaxed on a soft summer morning? Or was the wind howling and the fog swirling? Did his first hint that something was wrong come as a sickening shock and a horrible grinding as his hull went up on unyielding granite? Poor Barney. The coast is littered with landmarks like this . . . Barney's Mistake, Drunkard Ledge, so-and-so's Folly, somebody else's Despair, reminders that it is not always fun and games out here.

Along shore as we pass outside Buck Island and inside Spectacle I can see bits and pieces of a couple of monumental gray shingle cottages on a hillside, largely hidden by spruces all around. These are the classic old-time kind, all weathered wood, forest-green trim, and small-paned windows showing black. Vast yet comfortable looking, they appear to have taken care of generations of large families in a rambling space of wandering corridors, forgotten rooms, and maybe a ghost or two.

Spectacle Island to port is a smallish uninhabited place with sandy beaches and a small tuft of spruce at one end that almost qualifies as woods. Someone has placed a couple of serious-looking moorings in the lee as tie-ups for picnic visits no doubt. This looks like a spot where you could pick up one of those moorings for a day or two and have a really nice time just lying back. I know I will have this in mind next time *Penelope* and I pass this way.

We round Blake Point now, the northeast corner of Cape Rosier, and head in a northwesterly direction toward Head of the Cape. Reaching slowly along close to shore (the wind, what there is of it, has come around to the south), we pass a minor headland and come very near to a house with a large deck overlooking the water. Here I find that I have become unintentional party to an interesting domestic scene. Two young men and a girl are enjoying breakfast on the deck and, as a special treat to ancient mariners, the girl is topless. Not knowing quite what to do, I wave and they all wave back languidly, obviously unconcerned by my sudden intrusion.

I am reminded of an account by the English author and editor F. B. Cooke in his book *Pocket Cruisers*, published by Edward Arnold and Co., London, 1938. Cooke is describing a cruise he made in his first boat, the *Wave*, "way back in the 'nineties." He is tacking along shore near Clacton, a beach resort, when he finds himself so close in that he and his boat are "mixed up with the bathers." The result is that several bathing machine (a kind of waterborne beach cabana) doors are "hastily and violently slammed." Times change.

Borne away from this modern *Déjeuner sur l'herbe* by wind and tide, we soon find ourselves rounding Head of the Cape. Coming in our direction from out in East Penobscot Bay is a rather unusual-looking yawl built along more or less sharpie lines. She is unmistakable as a Phil Bolger creation. Looking farther out into the bay, I see that there is a whole procession of Bolger boats coming along.

This reminds me a little of the bar scene in *Star Wars*. They come in varying degrees of originality, from nearly normal looking to one in the distance that looks like a wedge of pie with a sail. Then there are a seaborne shoe and a yawl-rigged cigar. You have to hand it to America's (the world's?) boldest and most original boat designer, though. All these strange creations seem to work quite well. Friendly waves are exchanged and then we and the Bolger flotilla go our separate ways.

I am reminded that I almost owned a Bolger catboat myself at one time. A few years after getting back from Vietnam I was in the market for my first boat since boyhood and became enamored of a diminutive fourteen-foot Bolger-designed cruising catboat named *Lynx*. Of traditional plank-on-frame construction, she was the smallest boat to ever come off the ways at the famed Story shipyard. In the end I wound up with a twenty-one-foot French pocket cruiser, sister ship to the smallest finisher in one of the OSTAR races. That bulletproof little craft was a good choice and a great success, but I have always wondered what *Lynx* would have been like. I'd still like to try her.

Penelope runs northward now along the western shore of the cape.

We stay close inshore, enjoying the unrolling landscape and the diverse but uniformly opulent architecture along the way. Soon enough we are off the southernmost of the two entrances into Holbrook Island Harbor. We head in, broad reaching, and pass a twenty-seven- or twenty-eight-foot modern sloop along the way. I drink in their looks of surprise and irritation as we sweep by, and derive the usual immoderate, unseemly, and probably unwholesome satisfaction. I know it's not nice, but I just can't help it.

Somebody yells something indistinct from the dock as we race by the anchorage at the Holbrook Island Sanctuary. I can't make it out, but I think they are telling me I am headed for submerged rocks that make their way out from Ram Island, almost closing the passage to the northern end of the harbor. I know the way, though, having been here a couple of years before. Past the rocks we take a look at our old anchorage off the beach and find it attractive as ever.

It's still early, though, and we want to check out Smith Cove across a sandy isthmus, which looked good on our earlier visit. This means sailing out into the Bagaduce River, going upstream a way past the town of Castine on the north shore, and then hanging a right past Hospital Island and going into the cove. All this we do, but when we finally get there it is not nearly as appealing as our old anchorage so we reverse direction and sail all the way back to our old spot off the small curved beach. I soon realize that tonight the anchorage will not be mine alone as it was on the last visit. One after another the usual thirty-five- and forty-foot cruising boats arrive.

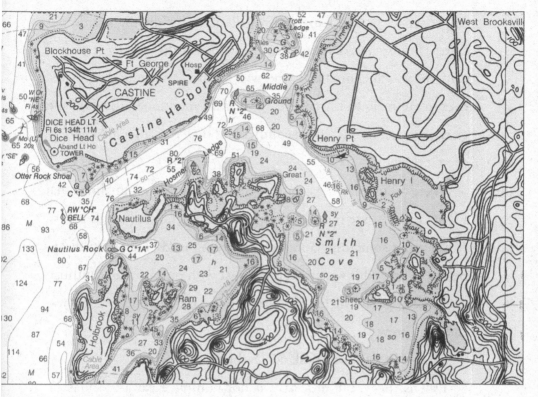

They are uniformly large, and I wonder again, as I have so many times before, where all the small cruisers are.

One of the arriving boats is a very shippy pocket schooner of a little over thirty feet, which I had encountered earlier in the summer. We had sighted each other coming out of the fog off North Haven Island and—apparently attracted by each other's good looks—had both altered course for a closer look and a word or two. Now I was anxious for an even closer look.

This was a fascinating little craft with nineteenth- or even eighteenth-century details like oaken water casks on deck. She lacked only gun ports and, of course, a little extra size to be something you might expect to find lying off Treasure Island while the murderous Israel Hands chased young Jim Hawkins up the rigging. I waited until she was anchored and otherwise squared away and then rowed over to say hello to the couple on board. I mentioned the date and circumstances of our first encounter and they remembered *Penelope* or said they did.

There followed a pleasant enough conversation but my hints that I would like to see more of their fascinating craft fell on deaf ears. Murmuring something about dinner being ready they soon disappeared below. This was in such contrast with our mutually enthusiastic exchanges in the fog off North Haven that I wondered if it was the same crew.

Thursday, Holbrook Island Harbor

Dawns foggy, but at least it is not raining. I eat a breakfast of eggs, bread, and a very dubious pork chop. Liberal lacings of soy

and Louisiana Hot Sauce cannot hide the fact that this one is well past its prime. Eating it at all may not be the best of ideas, but I survive. I am finding that my soy-soaked, bilge-cooled meats are not lasting as long as they used to. Can this be a function of global warming?

Eleven thirty a.m. brings zephyrs from the southeast. The fog inside the harbor has lifted, too, so we get under way and drift/sail out toward Nautilus Island and the open bay. Outside it is clear to the north toward Searsport, but I can see dense fog coming our way up the bay from seaward. Also coming our way are a couple of windjammers easing along in the light airs and headed up the bay. My plan today is to go north around the tip of Islesboro and then south down West Penobscot Bay with perhaps Gilkey Harbor as destination.

With the fog coming I heave to and spend a few minutes punch-

ing some new waypoints into the GPS: the north tip of Islesboro, the buoy off Belfast, a point off Gilkey Harbor, and another one off Camden. We should be well prepared if it is necessary to play blind man's bluff in West Penobscot Bay.

My only real concern about the day ahead is the possibility of meeting one of the occasional oil tankers that make their way up and down the bay en route to or from Searsport. This is the only serious commercial shipping in the area and I wouldn't care to encounter it in the fog in an engineless boat. If it is thick, I plan to hug one shore or another, where the big boys can't go.

The northern tip of Islesboro Island is called Turtle Head, and a glance at the chart shows you why. The whole northern end of the

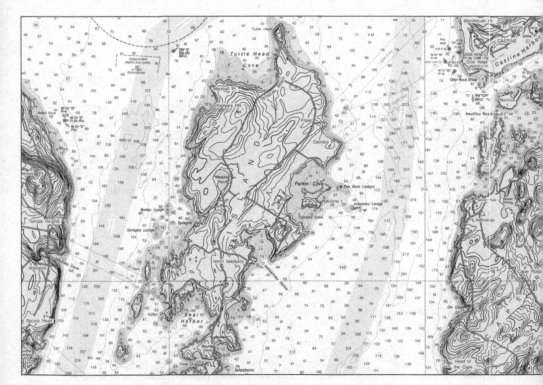

island is shaped like a turtle. It's not certain what kind because it has flippers to port and legs to starboard, but turtle it is, with a perfect head right to the north.

The fog has stalled somewhere down the bay and we approach Turtle Head in misty sunlight. We are moving at an appropriate turtle-like crawl with only enough wind to keep way on. It is not enough for a bulky thirty-five-footer close by and headed in the same direction. Her sails can't seem to catch anything at all and she is pretty much dead in the water.

This is a very unusual sight because most of these craft abandon sail and hit the starter button as soon as trying to sail is remotely inconvenient. Real sailors aboard this boat, I decide, and wave as we slowly pass. The crew is four very pleasant-looking ladies in their fifties. They are well groomed and, really, rather fragile looking. If I saw them in town, I would guess they were going to a tea party at the local parsonage. I ask them where they are headed, and they say they are on their way back home to Portsmouth, New Hampshire. I guess real sailors come in all sizes, shapes, and guises.

Passing close by Turtle Head and its distinctive vertical rock formations I notice a young couple sitting very close together in a small niche in the rock right at the uttermost tip of the island. I feel momentary pang of envy. I wish that I could be a young lover again. Probably they are wishing they had a beautiful little sailboat out on the bay.

Out in the middle of West Penobscot Bay the wind has picked up now. It is ten to fifteen knots from the southwest, right on our nose. The tide is coming in, too, so it is going to be a hard slog to get anywhere I want to go. Behind us the ladies from Portsmouth are sailing fast now, and I work hard, trying to stay ahead. We are separated by a mile or so and it is hard to tell if they are gaining.

The bay looks infinitely huge ahead, my possible objectives far away. The bloom has gone off the day, too, sunlight and color replaced by a uniform unpromising gray. Concentrating on sail trim and trying to get the best out of her while making so little tangible progress on this featureless gray expanse is turning into hard, not very pleasant work.

I consult the chart and see that we are off a couple of small islands, Seal and Flat, which themselves lie off a place called Seal Harbor. A look in Taft and Rindlaub reveals that Seal Harbor is adjacent to Crow Cove, described therein as "a little gunkhole where the crows are still there to greet you in the morning, and so are the seagulls and

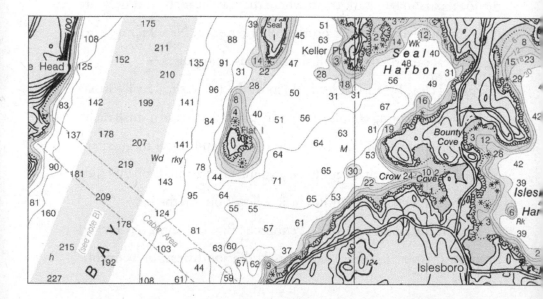

ospreys." Well, gunkholes with crows, seagulls, and ospreys are what I'm all about so, without further ado, I cut in between Seal and Flat and make my way toward the cove. As I approach land the sun comes out again and the wind becomes fluky, fitful gusts out of the east, again right on our nose. We get into the cove after some fits and starts in the narrow entrance, and find that it is indeed a sweet place.

The couple of houses in the area are set far enough back behind trees so you can't see them, and for the rest it is sandy shores, a rich green marsh, the crows, seagulls, and ospreys, along with a large population of friendly ducks that Taft and Rindlaub forgot to mention.

Friday, Crow Cove

Another bright morning finds me out in the dinghy exploring the shallows around the marsh in a sunny golden mist. Girls' voices and the thwunk of hard-hit tennis balls follow us as *Penelope* and I take our leave and head toward the bay. By eleven forty we are moving nicely southward along shore. The log reads: "This is sweet! We have southwest about seven knots but the bay is flat, showing only the tiniest of ripples. The land is a lush enticing green with splashes of gold. Everything else is shades of blue. Smooth sailing like on the banks in the Bahamas."

Off Gilkey Harbor at the south end of Islesboro we head in and pass close behind the ferry boat, which is loading, nuzzling against her slip with the engine running ahead. I am surprised at the force of the wash coming off her stern. *Penelope* is pushed violently sideward but shakes herself and continues to the east. Then it is south up between Islesboro and Seven Hundred Acre Island.

Onward to the south we go and find that we are caught in another almost endless beat. At last we reach the vicinity of Lime Island where it is possible to carry four feet between Lime and Lasell, and over into East Penobscot Bay. We gratefully cut through here and now head a little north of east passing between Great and Little Spruce Head Islands, summer home of the Porter family, the accomplished photographer and his equally talented brother the painter. We are reaching along at nearly hull speed and life is good again.

Late afternoon finds us off Pickering Island, a few miles from the west end of the Eggemoggin Reach. Pickering is uninhabited now but it was not always so, and there are some strange stories concerning days gone by.

A picture in Charles B. McLane's *Islands of the Mid-Maine Coast* shows an odd fortress-like building that stood here from some time in the 1890s until shortly after World War II. Looking like it might have made a good keep for Cedric the Saxon, it had a turret and barred windows on the second floor with no windows at all on the first. Protected in summer by a pack of ferocious dogs, this was the vacation home of a certain Dr. Collins.

Some said that the good doctor kept mental patients here for arcane experiments; others that he kidnapped bar girls in Boston and bought them out to the island for purposes too awful to contemplate. Still others said that the doctor was a perfectly nice fellow and all the evil rumors had been spread by a disgruntled clam digger.

On this night we share the western anchorage at Pickering with an older and somewhat worn-looking sloop that is anchored quite far out from the anchorage proper. She shows no lights and no signs of life. Vaguely, I wonder if there is a problem there, but assume the crew are early sleepers.

Saturday, Pickering Island

A gray windless morning. There are still no signs of life on the sloop but I figure they may be not only early sleepers, but late ones, too. I go for a long row along the shore, around to the eastern anchorage, which is off a beautiful curving sand beach. This place, one of the loveliest on the coast, is unoccupied as usual, the reason being a more or less treacherous rock-lined entrance and considerable ambiguity as to where the good bottom lies.

Back on *Penelope* I fry up some eggs and Spam and wonder about the old sloop, which still shows no sign of life. It's warm and with no company but the distant, lifeless sloop, I crouch low in the cockpit and take a seawater sponge bath. Other people say they still feel dirty after a seawater bath, but I have never felt that way; I like a little salt on my skin.

Light breezes stir and the day is getting along so I haul anchor and get under way. We pass close under the stern of the mystery sloop and hail her by name. I have no desire to find a dead man aboard, but feel duty-bound to check her out. To my great relief a gray head emerges from the hatch. I ask how he is doing and in a quavery old voice the old gent says that he is "just enjoying the

Pumpkin Island Light

peace." I apologize for disturbing that peace and wish him well. He opines that there is not likely to be much wind this afternoon, and I'm afraid he is right.

For an uncomfortable length of time, he is very right. We lay becalmed and drift slowly toward a rock off Scott Island. Things pick up at last and we are able to sail inside Pumpkin Island with its abandoned lighthouse and out into the reach.

All is well as we proceed eastward until we get to a point off the Benjamin River. Then we see thunderheads coming up behind us and it is a race to see if we can get to the WoodenBoat anchorage before the storm hits. Looking back toward the Deer Island Bridge, the sky is spectacular with flashes of blue, purple, and orange in the charcoal clouds.

It is "I think I can, I think I can" all the way up past Torrey Island and then we are in the anchorage. We drop anchor off the mooring field with a windjammer and a mixed bag of cruisers for company. We heave a big sigh of relief then note that what looked like a major thunderstorm has dissipated and disappeared while we were anchoring. It is time for a drink and a read in the cockpit.

I have been reading about Captain Nat Herreshoff and his last Cup defender. I come to a part which tells how he spent long days working at the Herreshoff Manufacturing Co., which he owned along with his brother. Coming home for dinner, he would preside over a table where his wife and children were discouraged from speaking because the great man preferred thinking about boats and boating undisturbed. After dinner, Captain Nat would retire to his study alone where he thought about boats and boating some more.

We gather Captain Nat was not a lot of fun as a husband and a father. Like so many great men and women, he was a bit selfish and difficult. (Frank Lloyd Wright, N. C. Wyeth, Robert Frost, Ayn Rand, and Picasso come to mind, to name just a few.) Suddenly it comes to me that my own days will end in obscurity because I have been too nice all my life . . . I can't suppress a sudden wild screech of laughter as I think about how my wife would react to this last idea. People in neighboring boats cast nervous glances in my direction. Clearly the old coot in the catboat is demented and may be dangerous.

Sunday, WoodenBoat, Brooklin

It is sunny and clear again as we beat out of the WoodenBoat Anchorage accompanied by a whole flotilla of wooden craft of all sizes. They seem to be headed for some kind of event on the other side of the reach. We part company off White Island as I head southeast for Jericho Bay and a clean shot for Hat Island, Toothacher Bay, and home. It's one tack with the sheet just slightly eased, and *Penelope* is doing five and a half to just under six knots.

A converted sardine carrier passes slowly headed slightly more to the west. Her skipper takes the trouble to step out of his wheelhouse and give the kind of exaggerated wave that indicates he really likes what he is seeing. It makes my day and tops off what has been a really fine cruise.

End of cruise: Hockamock Head Light at sundown.

19. Shemaya

Our house on Swan's Island sits right out at the tip of City Point at the head of Burnt Coat Harbor with water on three sides. A steep slope runs down to the shore covered with ferns, blackberries, bay-berries, a spruce or two, and a couple of ancient apple trees.

I was relaxing up on the porch on a misty, golden-hued August morning, enjoying all this along with my first cup of coffee, when I spied a strange craft emerging very slowly out of the mist.

There was no perceptible breeze and the small lugsail-rigged cat yawl was advancing at a rate that could only be called glacial. In fact it was hard to tell that she was moving at all.

A couple of things about this apparition claimed my whole at-tention right away.

First, visiting boats rarely venture up into our end of the harbor where the charts wrongly show two feet or less of water, so whoever was sailing this boat was more than usually adventurous. Second, the fact that the boat was sailing in virtually no wind meant there was a kindred spirit out there, someone who appreciated the subtle pleasures of winning one's way without recourse to crass mechanical measures.

Finally, there was the craft itself, a truly unusual vessel of nineteen feet or so, hard-chined, chunky, with a large multi-windowed house and smallish sails of novel cut. Not my idea of a beautiful boat perhaps, but a most interesting one and, for her length, probably quite useful. A boat that, to paraphrase the popular song, might not go very fast, but could go pretty far.

In short, I was intrigued by the whole business and determined that later in the day I must row out to meet this lone voyager whom I was sure would have many interesting things to show and tell.

It didn't work out, though. Part of the time the tide was wrong, and then I had a lot of other things that needed doing. Night came and I still hadn't been out to visit the mystery craft where she lay at anchor not far from *Penelope*. I resolved therefore to go out there first thing next morning. But at 6:30 a.m. next day, I looked out

into the harbor and found that our visitor had vanished as quietly
and as mysteriously as she had come.

I was sorry for the missed opportunity but thought no more
about it until a few days later at lovely Pickering Island, a favorite
anchorage not far from the western end of the Eggemoggin Reach.
I had just dropped anchor after a longish day of chasing zephyrs in
East Penobscot Bay. In plus or minus zero wind it had taken six
hours to traverse the few short miles between Orcutt Harbor and
the western anchorage at Pickering and I was ready for a drink.
There are moments, rare as they may be, when even I think an engine might be a useful piece of equipment.

Off in the distance a familiar form began to take shape. Slowly,
but with increasing certitude, I recognized the unusual profile of the
mysterious little yawl I had observed from my porch. And ever so
slowly she approached, moving with an almost magical inevitability
given that there was no perceptible wind or tide to propel her. She
arrived an hour or so later, and I was surprised to note that her single-handed skipper was not some grizzled old sea dog like myself
but an attractive blond woman, probably somewhere in her forties
or fifties.

This was news indeed, for single-handed female sailors are about
as rare as the proverbial hen's teeth. Given all my previous interest
and speculation, I was now doubly interested in going to talk to her.
But a wily old salt on a vintage powerboat, the only other craft in
the anchorage, was faster. In no time at all he was out in a little green

kayak, circling around and chattering away like a magpie. I decided to leave the evening chat to him and try again in the morning. I did get to talk to her the next day, and what a story she had to tell.

Shemaya Laurel learned sailing and a love of being on the water as a teenager during summer vacations with her grandmother, who lived in Stonington on the Connecticut shore of Long Island Sound. She had an O'Day Widgeon there, and long days afloat laid the foundation for what she would always be, first and last: a sailor.

The cares and obligations that come along in the course of everybody's lives kept her away from the water except for occasional day sailing during her twenties and thirties. Complicating her situation during this period was the onset of more or less debilitating symptoms of Lyme disease, which for a time made sailing completely impossible. But at forty she bought a Bristol Corsair 24 and came back to the sport with a vengeance. Cruising in the lower Connecticut River and Long Island Sound was interspersed with intense home study on all aspects of navigation and small boat cruising.

After a year or two of this, Shemaya moved up to a classic Lyle Hess–designed Falmouth Cutter. As aficionados know, this hefty twenty-two-footer is probably the ultimate pocket yacht with accommodations, sea keeping abilities, a turn of speed to match many much larger boats, and a jaunty, salty look that can bring tears to your eyes (especially if, like me, you want, but can't manage to have, one).

Thus equipped, Shemaya set out to do some serious cruising.

The years 2002 and 2003 saw a couple of cruises Down East from Connecticut, the more ambitious one being a two-and-a-half-month affair that got as far as Cutler, Maine, up by the Canadian border where the fog swirls especially thick, the tides are extreme, and the current runs hard. As skipper of a splendid craft with time and impaired but sufficient strength at her disposal, it seemed the sky was the limit. Almost any sailing ambition was within reach.

But then the pernicious microbe asserted itself again and Shemaya's condition spiraled downward to a point where sailing was no longer an option. There followed three years during which Shemaya and various helpers were occupied in finding, if not a cure, at least a modus vivendi, a way of living with a disease that can be subdued to some degree but will not go away.

At last Shemaya was ready to sail again, but it could not be the same. The Falmouth Cutter with its large sail area and heavy rig was now too much boat for her. Weakened to the point that walking was difficult and even getting on and off, up and down on that high-sided craft was not practical, trying to single-hand the boat on long cruises was out of the question. But sail she would. Shemaya sold the cutter and got herself a fourteen-foot Peep Hen micro-cruiser and continued logging sea miles. Even in that tiny craft she and a friend managed a cruise from Danversport, Massachusetts, to Kittery on the coast of Maine.

In 2008 Shemaya commissioned the building of her present craft, the nineteen-foot-eight-inch Bolger-designed "Chebacco boat" *Auklet*, perhaps with the idea of finding a compromise between the Falmouth Cutter (which was too big) and the Peep Hen (which was too small).

The *Auklet* was launched in April 2012 and Shemaya has been on board pretty much ever since. Most people for whom even the simple process of getting on and off boats can involve pain and difficulty would probably call it a day and elect to stay off boats. Shemaya's solution has been to stay *on* the boat most of the time, and it works for her. She seems happy and relaxed on board her floating home, and is proud of leaving a very light footprint on her environment. *Auklet* is equipped with solar panels for power, and a composting toilet for zero impact on her surroundings. Shemaya is even experimenting with growing some of her own vegetables on board.

Throughout her various tribulations, Shemaya's attitude has remained relentlessly upbeat. In an earlier draft of this article I referred to the onset of Lyme disease as "a disaster." Shemaya objected to this, saying that she prefers to think of it as an opportunity to "learn many new things." She sees life as an adventurous journey in which you take the cards you are dealt and always try to make the most of them.

While *Auklet* is seldom seen under anything but wind power, she does have a Torqeedo 1003 electric outboard that Shemaya uses only very sparingly, and only in situations that might otherwise become dangerous. She says she considers the outboard as "training wheels" for going engineless, which she hopes to do in the near future. A yuloh is under consideration but she is not sure she would be strong enough to use it successfully. Meanwhile the simple process of waggling the rudder back and forth has provided sufficient propulsion for many windless situations.

The boat—which technically is Bolger's Chebacco #2 design, or "Glass House Chebacco" (see *Boats with an Open Mind* by Phillip C. Bolger, International Marine, 1994)—was drawn and built as a gaff-headed cat yawl with considerably more sail area than she shows now, but somewhere around launch time the original mast delaminated and rather than wait around for repairs, Shemaya took a shorter mast from another boat and improvised the lug-rigged main. I mentioned that a junk-rigged main of greater area might be ideal for both her and the boat and she said that indeed she had been thinking about it. I mentioned Blondie Hasler's book on the junk rig (a very obscure reference indeed) and she said that oh yes, she had a copy. This led to a general discussion of the literature of the sea and cruising in particular from which I came away believing that she has read most all of it, if not everything.

During the course of our conversation, I mentioned to Shemaya that I occasionally wrote for *Points East* and other publications and asked if she would send me a copy of her itinerary for the summer of 2012 so folks would know what a small boat and a determined sailor can really do. It follows below. I can only say that it reads more like the index to a cruising guide for New England waters than a description of a single cruise.

Auklet 2012 Shakedown Cruise Itinerary

April 20, Deep River, Connecticut—first launch
Twenty days at Warren's dock in Deep River, with side-trip test run for two
   nights in Selden Creek, across the Connecticut River from Deep River—
   fitting out
Middle of May
Madison, Connecticut, at friend's dock in the Neck River until May 31—
   more fitting out
Fishers Island
Stonington, Connecticut
Point Judith Pond
Month of June
Narragansett Bay, Dutch Harbor, Wickford
Sakonnet River
Cuttyhunk
Narragansett Bay again, rudder post/tiller connection repair
Cuttyhunk again
Going back and forth including Sakonnet Harbor, Westport Harbor, and
   third beach in the Sakonnet River two or three times
Departing Cuttyhunk eastbound
First few days of July
Onset Harbor, shore support meeting for supplies, and waiting for favorable
   timing of tide
July 5, Cape Cod Canal transit
Wellfleet outer harbor (two nights)

Sesuit Harbor, East Dennis (two nights)

Duxbury/Plymouth (three nights)

Rockport

Isles of Shoals

Stage Island Harbor, Cape Porpoise (two nights)

Wood Island Harbor, Biddeford (two nights)

Jewell Island, Casco Bay

South Freeport (three nights)

Little Whaleboat Island, Casco Bay

Cliff Island, Casco Bay

Damariscove Island

Christmas Cove, Damariscotta River (three nights)

Poorhouse Cove, John's River (three nights)

Pemaquid Harbor

Shark Island, Muscungus Bay (desperation anchorage—not recommended)

Long Cove, Tenants Harbor

Lyman Morse slip, Tenants Harbor—shore support

Long Cove

Birch Island, Muscle Ridge

North Haven, shallow cove immediately south of Pulpit Harbor entrance

August 14, Buck's Harbor

Greenlaw Cove, Deer Isle

Swans Island

White Islands, Hurricane Sound (three nights)

Pickering Island

Holbrook Island Cove, Castine

Belfast (three days)

Holbrook Island Cove, Castine (two nights)

Great Spruce Head Island, north of North Haven

Birch Island, Muscle Ridge (two nights)

Long Cove, Tenants Harbor

Turkey Cove, St. George River

Love Cove, Ebencook Harbor, Sheepscot River

Rounded Cape Small midafternoon, wind went away, hard to get into harbor, decided to sail all night, and then most of next day; next anchorage was Little Harbor, Portsmouth New Hampshire (five nights)

Another long day

Manchester by the Sea, Massachusetts (four nights)

September 20

Cape Ann Marina, Annisquam River, Gloucester (two nights), then Dave Zeiger (the Triloboats guy) and Anke Wagner come aboard for several days

Looking back at all this, no wonder I'm tired!

As of this writing (spring 2015) Shemaya is still hard at it. She continues to voyage up and down the East Coast like a shuttlecock, and now owns a house in far eastern Maine. She has recently installed a junk rig on the *Auklet*. With considerably larger sail area, we expect she will be going faster and farther than ever. Shemaya publishes a blog of her ongoing adventures which can be found by Googling "Sailing Auklet."

20. Penelope's Bag of Tricks

Wednesday, August 16, dawns clear and crisp. In the a.m. I ferry supplies out to *Penelope* on her mooring off our house on City Point, Burnt Coat Harbor. The breeze is brisk from the northwest, not our favorite direction—most anyplace we want to go will be to windward—but we will take it.

This is one of those crystal-clear nor'wester days when the sea turns almost black and the leaves on the trees along shore turn up in the wind, showing their whitish undersides.

I decide to tie in a reef before we go. If the nor'wester is brisk in the harbor, it will be truly boisterous outside, a rule I have learned over and over.

I take off the sail ties and let the tanbark sail lie along the deck as I haul in the reefing lines at tack and clew. Since we are still on the mooring and at our leisure, I also tie in the reef points along the sail. This last is more cosmetic than necessary. When reefing single-handed under way, I seldom have time for it.

Reef all Bristol fashion, the sail goes up. The throat and peak halyards are hauled up together until the luff is fully extended. We then belay the peak halyard and swig up the throat halyard good and tight. We want a good taut luff. Then the peak halyard is hauled on up until a pronounced vertical crease appears in the sail. After the topping lift has been eased, the crease disappears, and the sail sets nicely.

The sheet is almost all the way out as it has been since the sail started to go up. This allows her to jill back and forth while spilling enough wind so that she does not try to sail over the mooring.

Now we wait until, sail slatting, she falls off in the desired direction. Then we run forward, uncleat the mooring pendant, and walk it back along the windward rail to the cockpit, where we drop it overboard. She forereaches slowly till I put the helm down, then starts off downwind.

Going downharbor we are broad reaching, almost running, so the sheet stays out and the board stays up.

We run past the visiting yachts at anchor, past the Lobster Co-op, and past the lovely schooner *Mary Day*, which is preparing to make sail, then round Hockamock Head and out into Jericho Bay.

Now we are headed north up the bay. The board goes down and the sheet comes in.

The tide is ebbing, so as we head up the bay close-hauled, we face a hard slog against both wind and tide. *Penelope* is a powerful sailer, though, and it is good to feel her fight and win her way. I help her out by avoiding the middle of the bay between Swan's and Marshall Islands where the outgoing tide runs hardest. By watching the lobster buoys closer to shore, I can see where the current weakens, and use that to help her along.

An hour and change sees us up by Hat Island and parallel with the north end of Marshall. Here the plan is to bear slightly to port and head west for Merchants Row and Deer Isle. But now the wind falls light, and I busy myself with shaking out the reef as we drift slowly back the way we have come.

Reef all shaken out, she drifts, sail flapping, on a glassy sea. If this keeps up, the one- or two-knot current will deliver us back to the harbor in an hour or two. It's frustrating, but the engineless sailor learns patience. I think of anchoring to save distance made while we wait for wind, but then, thrilling sight, off in the distance the water darkens perceptibly. Wind is on its way. We watch the darkness spread and grow, coming closer. It's better than watching a good movie.

South-southwest it is now, and we are off again. This is a more favorable slant that gets us past the Halibut Rocks and grassy, bird-bedecked Southern Mark Island on one tack. Here we fall off and reach northwest around McGlathery Island to the snug anchorage between McGlathery and Round. These are wildly beautiful uninhabited islands with a sad history.

McGlathery was home to a thriving small community until a time in the 1800s when a diphtheria epidemic swept the area. Within a week all fourteen children resident on the island were dead, and the surviving adults soon left for other shores. Sometime around then the wife of the island's earliest and leading settler committed suicide, most likely for reasons having to do with these grim events.

Now the island is home only to seabirds and some occasional sheep. A few gravestones, some tumbledown stone walls, and a few scraps of old iron in the woods are the only evidence of those earlier times.

As usual there are several large yachts in the anchorage ranging from thirty-five to around fifty feet. As usual, *Penelope* will have to assume her role of poor relation, lone small craft among a fleet of opulent giants.

Sometimes, and this is surely one of them, we feel nostalgic for the days before the GPS came into general use. Then visitors to these fogbound shores were considerably more rare. The boats one did encounter tended to be smaller, more traditional and, frequently, made out of wood. The appliance most often seen in action was the woodstove, not the TV, air conditioner, or microwave.

Penelope gets nervous glances as she sails in among the fleet, looking for a spot to drop the hook. Anchoring under sail is a practice that pretty much went out of style in these parts along with the woodstove, and it is clear that some of our new neighbors regard it as reckless.

I see our spot and close reach toward it. With a few yards to go I let the sheet run and go forward to handle the anchor. You want the anchor to hit bottom while there is still some way on so it will set when you snub her up. I let out chain and rode, then take a turn around the mooring cleat. The anchor digs in, stops her, and she begins to round up. Then it is back to the cockpit to swig up the topping lift, lower the gaff to near horizontal, then let go the twin halyards for throat and peak, and the gaff and sail come rushing down into the lazy jacks just as she comes into the wind.

These operations go smoothly, as they sometimes will, and we look pretty good.

All of this, if possible, is accomplished at the "schoonerman's gait"—which is quick because it has to be, but looks deceptively slow and deliberate, which is cool. The schoonermen of old were masters at this, doing everything with apparently insouciant ease. We can only emulate it to a degree.

Note that the way not to anchor or pick up a mooring on a catboat would be to come right up into the wind and then go forward. First you would thereby lose the headway you need to set the hook; worse, you would find yourself on your tiny foredeck just when the boom will want to come over. Catboats are playful things and one of their favorite tricks is to catch you on the foredeck and push you right overboard with the boom.

At anchor, I have time just before sunset to enjoy a glass of wine in the cockpit and study the mores and folkways of our affluent neighbors. This is only fair because I know they are busy studying our mores and folkways, too.

When sailors are not actually sailing, much of their time is given over to enjoying the mistakes, mishaps, and foibles of other sailors. There is definitely more than a touch of schadenfreude to this cockpit-borne recreation. Who can claim not to have been entertained by classics like the oft-repeated comedy of the choleric, wildly gesticulating skipper and the hapless, flustered trophy wife at anchoring time? It's certainly not nice, but we all do it.

On this evening I get a kick out of a fellow who descends from his massive trawler yacht into his Zodiac-type dinghy, where he spends ten minutes struggling with a balky outboard. When, sweaty and red-faced from his efforts, he finally gets her fired up, he proceeds only a few short yards to a neighboring yacht where he promptly ties up again. He could have simply drifted over there in a fraction of the time. A friend of mine once observed that many of these people have rowing machines at home, but while they will row away for hours in an exercise room, it never occurs to them to do so on the water.

Thursday, August 17. Another beautiful bell-clear morning. The enticing smell of frying bacon drifts over a peaceful anchorage. I am experiencing considerably more fellow-feeling for my neighbors than

I was on the night before. If they have chosen to expend the energy and expense necessary to be in this magical place on this exquisite morning, they can't be all bad.

We are lying close to some rocks off Round Island and somewhat hemmed in by boats farther out. On an early-morning exploration in the dinghy I noted that there was a lot of good water up toward the head of the anchorage. The big boats have been conservative in their anchoring practice, leaving a big hole up there in what is otherwise a tightly packed harbor.

I want that extra room as I sail off the anchor. However well you know your boat, sailing off the anchor in close proximity to other boats has its risks. There is a chance, however slight, that your boat will somehow manage to go off on the wrong tack, with trouble and embarrassment to follow. Catboats, in particular, indulge in these occasional pranks just to keep you honest.

Noting that wind and tide are both flowing toward the open water, I simply lift the hook a small way off the bottom and drift back to the desired spot. I have an oar ready, but there is no need. I lower the hook again and prepare to make sail.

Penelope has a short bowsprit and our main anchor rides there in a stainless-steel roller on the starboard side. This is a twenty-pound CQR with fifteen feet of extra-heavy chain and two hundred feet of nylon rode. This is a good combination for this boat, not too heavy for a single-hander to handle easily, but heavy enough to be generally reliable. Adding a twenty-five-pound sentinel when conditions look dubious makes it pretty bulletproof.

It's almost impossible to carry too many anchors on a cruising sailboat, and the prudent mariner will bring along more than is usually considered adequate. This goes double for an engineless boat.

Penelope carries twenty- and twenty-five-pound CQRs, and twenty-five- and thirty-five-pound fisherman anchors. There has been more than one time when we were glad we had them all.

The chain and the rode go over the roller on the sprit and back to the cockpit from whence I can haul anchor in comfort and safety, leaving *Penelope* with no chance to play her mischievous little game of "send the skipper for a swim."

I pull in rode until I can just feel the chain begin to lift off the bottom. Then, with the sheet way out, the sail goes up. Now I ease the topping lift, wait for her to fall over onto the desired tack, quickly get in the rest of the rode and chain, and we are off.

Once under way, and clear of neighboring boats, I go forward to wrestle the anchor up onto its roller and rinse off some mud.

We then proceed up between Round and Wreck Islands where we have the unusual experience (for Maine waters) of speaking another catboat. A spiffy little eighteen-footer, a Marshall Sanderling, I think, is running down toward us from Crotch Island way.

We tack over to have a word. She is manned by another single-hander and a very large black dog. I ask where they hail from, but, being a little hard of hearing, don't get it. Somewhere west and south anyway. I ask how the dog likes catboating and get back, "He tolerates it." I think of my own brace of English setters and wish I could have them along. But setters are not sea dogs, as several of my present pair's antecedents have proven to me most emphatically.

I think of Sherlock, a competent and athletic bird dog who became a goofy clown whenever he got near the water and a boat. In the dinghy he would assume heroic poses reminiscent of Washington crossing the Delaware. Then, invariably, with a pathetic yelp, he would contrive to fall overboard. Once rescued, he would guard his wetness like a treasure until he could worm his whole dripping carcass into my bunk. Sherlock was a lot of fun to have along, but an endless rainy week during which he did his best to keep everything sopping wet cost him his ticket.

Farther along this same short stretch of water there is a sturdy Tahiti Ketch improbably anchored in the middle of the fairway. Deep water, no shelter, a snug anchorage right around the corner . . . strange. A lone figure is standing disconsolately by the mizzen.

"Nice boat," I say as I sail by.

"Thank you," comes back a woman's voice, a little shaky, I think.

Various scenarios run through my head. Perhaps she has murdered her man, and he lies sprawled in a pool of blood on the cabin sole, or perhaps she has been abducted by pirates, and cowers on deck while they sleep off a drunken stupor below. Something here is definitely off key.

I wonder if she might really be in some kind of trouble, but, if so, she's had every chance to say something as we passed, so we continue on our way.

We sail inside Farrel Island being careful to avoid the half-tide rock, which comes out a long way from Crotch Island, and on past Mark Island Light. I note that bearings given by compass and GPS vary by about twelve degrees here, something to check on later (subsequent inquiries reveal that there are reported but unconfirmed magnetic anomalies in this area).

The GPS is a new addition. In younger days I always felt confident in fog with only a compass, a patent log, and my senses. Detecting the proximity of land by the sudden spicy smell of spruce, or knowing that you were sailing under the lee of an island when you sailed from cool air into warm, was the very cream of the sport. The sound of breaking water seemed an ample warning of rocks ahead. It was, by the way, counterproductive to use an engine very much because you immediately lost the use of two vitally important senses, sound and smell.

Older and either wiser or more timid now, I find the GPS to be a magical thing. Like the character in the Kafka story who keeps adding new escape routes to his burrow until he realizes there are now too many ways for an enemy to get in, I have added a second GPS to my gear. What if the first one quits just when I need it most? Do I need a third, or how about a nice big chart plotter?

We are headed for Islesboro Harbor on Islesboro Island where a marine artist friend from Swan's Island is about to have a show of recent works. Sailing over to show support is this week's excuse for going cruising.

The way is now clear to run up Penobscot Bay with a nice following breeze. The board has been up since shortly after I passed the Tahiti Ketch, and I won't need it again today.

Penelope flies along the Deer Island shore, past Sheep and Bald Islands to port. Past the Porcupines and past Eagle Island Light. I watch a nice wooden ketch anchor off the sandy beach on Eagle and decide that someday I want to do the same.

On past Butter Island we go. Once home to a grand hotel, the island is deserted now, a haunting place of grassy meadows, wooded slopes, and incredibly beautiful tidal bars nearby. (Sadly this description from a few years back no longer quite fits. Somebody has built an imposing house right at the very top of the highest hill on the island. It now dominates what had been a wild and unbroken land- and seascape for many miles around.)

Our course veers slightly to the west now, and we race on past Beach and Pond Islands toward Hewes Point on Islesboro Island, which marks Islesboro Harbor. I note that the point is easy to pick out along the Islesboro shore—a darker spot in the encompassing green—even from as far away as Butter Island.

At 4:30 p.m. we drop anchor in Islesboro Harbor. This is pretty much an open roadstead, fine in the prevailing southwesterlies, but questionable in south winds, and bad in those from east, southeast, northeast, and north. Thus I determine to row out a second anchor. I like a second anchor anyway.

I lay the twenty-five-pound CQR and its chain in the bottom of the dinghy and drop a laundry basket with a couple of hundred feet of coiled rode in on top of it. Then with the bitter end of the line made fast to the mooring cleat, I row out at about a forty-five-degree angle to the first anchor and drop the second hook.

Today we have adhered to a rule that we try never to ignore in a place like this, which is liable to become a dangerous lee shore. To wit, you should never anchor too near shore. A boat that begins to drag while anchored too close in will not have the time or distance necessary to successfully deploy more anchors. Helpless, it will be driven back to various degrees of disaster on shore.

Our thoughts turn to dinner. Tonight steak and Boston baked beans are on the menu. Nothing could be finer, at least not after a day of sun, wind, and water.

I start each cruise with several large frozen steaks, which are stored in the cool bilge. When the steaks thaw after a day or two, I soak them in soy sauce and place them in plastic containers, which go back into the bilge.

You can keep beef up to a week in this way, and it tastes better at the end of that time than it does in the beginning. Fresh vegetables like peas, beans, spinach, and tomatoes are good shipmates, and last quite well on short voyages. Frozen, boiled potatoes will provide a supply of home fries for a while.

Heavily represented in our larder are cans of skinless and boneless sardines in olive oil, and, above all, Spam.

Poor Spam. Surely this is one of the world's least understood and most seriously underappreciated bounties. The Russians acknowledged that our shipments of Spam during World War II were a major factor enabling them to survive the Nazi onslaught, but why, they rather churlishly wanted to know, did we have to send so much? Among the rare folk who actually admit to liking the stuff are Solomon Islanders who say it is the closest they can get to human flesh in these difficult and politically correct times.

Well, I like Spam, especially on boats. Fried Spam and eggs is a great way to start the day. Then there is spaghetti carbonara made with finely diced, crisply fried Spam. Finally, a mixture of scrambled eggs, fresh sautéed mussels, herbs, and diced fried Spam makes a dish that rises to gourmet standards. Friends of mine have found it quite wonderful until I tell them what is in it.

Friday, August 18. Another bluebird day. Bright sunshine and light southwest breezes. A very pleasant gentleman comes rowing by, taking his morning exercise. I can tell that he likes *Penelope*, and this is confirmed when he offers me the use of his private dock nearby. My benefactor later offers me an automobile tour of the island and is the first of several people at Islesboro who go out of their way to be kind and helpful.

After breakfast, I row ashore to check out my friend's exhibit at the local historical society. Along the way I am astonished to see a nicely equipped and well-kept public tennis court. I reflect that affluent people "from away" must have gained appreciable influence over local politics here. Home on Swan's Island a public tennis court would be about as unlikely a sight as a flying lobster.

Because the art exhibit opening is scheduled for this evening, I figure my friend and his wife will be busy hanging pictures and arranging lights. But after the two-mile walk to the site, I find that all this work has been done, and my friends are nowhere to be found.

I leave a note and walk another couple of miles to the busy island store, where I buy some beautiful, locally grown spinach and a warm, fragrant slice of pizza as fuel for the walk back to the boat. The store also lets me use their phone for a call to Swan's Island at no charge.

No sooner am I on my way than a pickup truck stops and another helpful islander insists on taking me all the way back to the dock, which is more than a mile out of his way.

Back on the boat, the weather radio is making dire predictions about the weather to come. Thirty to thirty-five knots out of the southeast for the next couple of days. Islesboro Harbor will be an uneasy place in those conditions, so I must cut short my visit and head for better shelter.

Leaving an anchorage can be more complicated if you have two anchors out. If the boat has swung around her anchors in wind and tide, the rodes will have twisted around each other, and, thus entwined, they can be difficult to separate. This is one reason *Penelope's* anchor rodes are all kept coiled in plastic laundry baskets (look for the simple, well-ventilated, bucket-sized number that Walmart sells for about four dollars). Thus, when your lines are twisted, you need only take one of the baskets forward and hand it around the other line until they are no longer foul.

As mentioned previously, this system also greatly facilitates rowing out and/or retrieving second anchors. Letting go from deck works better, too, because the rode uncoils freely with never a kink, snarl, or hang-up. The more usual procedure of pulling line up from below through the narrow bronze fixture standard on most boats is just asking for trouble. And feeding line back down that same hole after the anchor is up is just a boring waste of time.

A final piece of gear useful in bringing up the second anchor is my (alas, unpatented) dinghy stern roller. You go out to your anchor in the dinghy by pulling hand over hand on the rode and coiling it in its basket as it comes aboard. When you are over the anchor, you lay the rode over the transom-mounted roller, sit back on the thwart, and pull in line from a seated position in the middle of the boat. Your purchase is vastly improved, and you are not inviting a swamping by hanging out over the transom. The roller is the bow roller from a small boat trailer and can be found at any marine supplier.

Anchor up and sheet eased, we reach away from Islesboro Harbor in a fifteen-knot southwest breeze. East across the bay lies historic Castine, central to early New England history (see the novels of Kenneth Roberts or read the descriptions in Alf Loomis's classic cruising yarn *Ranging the Maine Coast*), and an architectural showplace, full of classic frame structures from earlier times, all meticulously maintained.

Penelope flies across the bay in what is now a reefing breeze, but we don't reef. The distance, only six or seven miles, is too short, and I am feeling lazy.

A popular platitude, verging on cliché, vis-à-vis reefing a catboat, goes that the time to reef a catboat is when you first think about it. This may make some sense around Vineyard Sound and Buzzards Bay where the breeze is likely to be brisk in early afternoon, brisker still by midafternoon, and even stronger later on. But here in Maine the pattern is different.

Afternoon breezes wax and wane in a much more unreliable pattern. If you reef when you first think of it you will likely be shaking it out shortly thereafter. If you continue along these lines, you may be reefing and unreefing all day. My conclusion has been that you reef not when you first think about it, but only when you really need to.

Now, while we certainly should be thinking about reefing, *Penelope* must be making quite a picture with spray flying and the dinghy trying to get airborne. I notice that we are being filmed from a Hinckley yawl. I wave, and they wave back enthusiastically.

Soon enough we reach the slot between Nautilus and Holbrook Islands near the mouth of the Bagaduce River. Although I want to visit Castine, I don't want to spend the night in the crowded anchorage there, where it can be noisy and uneasy from the considerable maritime traffic. Besides, I need clean seawater for my stainless-steel pot and whatever dinner will be.

Fortunately for misanthropes and nature lovers, there are several really nice anchorages just across the river. I have chosen Holbrook Island Harbor, well protected, lightly used, and surrounded by a nature preserve.

Penelope roars in past the can off Nautilus Island and finds herself once again in flat water though the wind is, if anything, still piping up. I am a bit irked to see that there is a genuine mega yacht (the kind that looks like a miniature ocean liner, replete with uniformed crew, starlets, certified billionaires, and constantly running generators) anchored off Ram Island in the middle of the harbor.

A voice in my head is silently screaming, *Go back to the Côte d'Azure where you belong*, as we scud by. Curmudgeon in a dudgeon, one might say. A couple of crew members wave pleasantly from a lofty deck and I return their salute. My argument, if I legitimately have one at all, is not with them.

Fortunately Holbrook Island Harbor is a large body of water, and by the time I reach my chosen spot off on the eastern side, we are far enough from the Onassis look-alike that we won't hear his generator or smell his diesel fumes.

I drop anchor off a small curving sand beach and life is not so bad after all. Gulls squabble on the nearby shore, and a lone osprey wheels high overhead unleashing his shrill intermittent cry.

Yes, life is good. I'm pretty sure I'll find something good to eat in the galley below, and the wine steward assures me that there is no shortage of Côtes du Rhône.

It's time to try a phone call home. It works, and I am able to assure my long-suffering spouse that I have not been waylaid by some island Circe, nor eaten by a Cyclops in his gruesome cave.

Sunday, August 19, dawns gray and chill. A leisurely breakfast of coffee, Spam, and eggs, and I am off in the dinghy bound for the bright lights of Castine. It's a good row of a mile or two, and in my new, shapely eight-and-a-half-foot dinghy *Argos*, with good bronze oarlocks and properly sized oars, I thoroughly enjoy it. (Argos was Odysseus's dog who, along with Penelope, awaited the hero's return.)

Rowing has gone out of fashion, and, while it has, the available equipment has tended to become degraded also. It's no wonder fewer and fewer people want to row when they have never had a chance to try a good rig. Shallow plastic or potmetal oarlocks, stubby oars, and fat, tubby boats just don't make for a good time.

Arriving at Castine's crowded town dock, I regret not having a camera to make a shot of the massed yacht tenders assembled there. It is just wall-to-wall Zodiac-type inflatables, each and every one with an outboard motor.

I take advantage of the only good thing about inflatables, which is that they can't scratch up your topsides, and wedge *Argos* between a pair of fat, rubbery ugly ducklings and step onto the dock.

First stop is a bakery/delicatessen overlooking the harbor. Breakfast number two is a world-class petit pain au chocolate and more good coffee. There are some really nice boats to look at out in the harbor, not least among them a graceful white Alden-designed raised-deck ketch that is just coming into the docks.

I pay my bill and begin a leisurely tour of town where each successive architectural masterpiece is trumped by the next, all in the serene shade of the many towering American elms that still survive here.

Wandering past the Maine Maritime Academy, I see the academy football team practicing on a freshly limed field. This being a Saturday, I wonder if there will be a game this afternoon, so early in the season. Another onlooker tells me that, no, football games take place in the autumn, and gives me one of those looks reserved for the silly or the simple-minded.

Suitably chastened, I'm back on *Penelope* in the early afternoon, having made additional stops at the grocery store and a bookshop.

I've bought John Vigor's account of his family's emigration from South Africa in a small yacht, and it turns out to be a good read. Previously I had read his *Twenty Small Boats That Will Take You Anywhere*, which is a must for any want-to-be small voyager, as is Stan Grayson's *Sailing Small*.

During the afternoon I take a long, low-tide row around Holbrook Island Harbor, partly recreation, and partly prospecting to check out the western route back to East Penobscot Bay. This looks tricky on the chart because of extensive submerged rocks that make out a long way from Ram Island toward the Holbrook shore, but once you have seen them at low tide, there is no problem.

Sunday, August 20. "Rain," said the forecast, and rain it is. There is a south wind predicted for twenty to twenty-five knots, exactly wrong for our planned run to North Haven Island. Attempting the passage in these conditions sounds altogether too rigorous and unrewarding. Like the schoonermen of old we will "wait our chance." The art of engineless sailing has much to do with being smart enough to avoid banging your head against a wall.

Fortunately I have the Vigor book, so today will be for reading and more rowing. I try hiking some of the trails in the nature preserve, but the mosquitoes are unbelievably fierce in this damp weather and I flee back to the dinghy. I won't even stop for an extensive patch of succulent chanterelle mushrooms I spy along the path. I would be eaten alive before I could gather even a few.

Monday, August 21. Light rain showers and a soft northwest

breeze. Quite pleasant really. We get under way by ten thirty and ghost in a southwesterly direction along the Cape Rosier shore. This is one of my favorite kinds of sailing, just ghosting along in perfect silence.

The light drizzle is pleasantly cool and the shore seems shrouded in a misty dream-like trance. The wind dies and we drift aimlessly, still well short of Penobscot Bay. I use the oars occasionally to keep her in the middle of the channel.

An hour passes and then patience is rewarded by a steady ten knots from the north-northwest. I aim *Penelope* over toward the Islesboro shore. My hoped-for goal today is Pulpit Harbor on North Haven, which is south down the bay, but I want to sightsee along the Islesboro shore as we go.

We have a pleasant enough run along the island, but the scenery (stately summer homes of the rich) is less interesting to me than if it was purely natural or if it revealed the abodes of seafarers and fishermen. Somewhere along the way, the sun breaks out and steam rises from the wet decks and my clothing.

All too soon Pulpit Rock looms ahead. We are at anchor in the snug harbor behind it by two in the afternoon. Given the time of day and the perfect breeze, I would have liked to go on down the island shore to make the always interesting passage through the Fox Island Thoroughfare, but I am hoping to pick up some oysters from my friend Adam Campbell.

Alas, a voice on the phone informs me that Adam is off island at a family affair somewhere and there is no one available to harvest oysters for me. This is a major disappointment but I'll have to live with it. Meanwhile we are faced with a pleasant afternoon in one of the best and most beautiful harbors on the coast.

Things could be worse.

Tuesday, August 22. Bright sun and a cloudless sky. I row around to the narrow bight where the Cabots keep their fleet. Over in one corner is an ancient Crowninshield Knockabout that I visit every year. She oozes turn-of-the-century charm and, as expected, I am charmed anew. Another corner is home to a graceful gunning dory, which unassuming as she is may be the most perfectly exquisite craft we have seen on this cruise.

Under way just before 10 a.m. we caper and dance our way down the north side of North Haven until we run out of wind and find ourselves adrift off Sheep Island. The colors here are incredibly vibrant in the crystal air, the island-dotted seascape of brilliant green gems on a royal-blue field, beautiful, and I, for one, have no problem with just lying back with a cold beer and enjoying the sun.

Half an hour of this and then the breeze picks up and builds steadily. We fly over toward Stonington on Deer Isle with a nice boost from the tide. By the time we are between Farrel and Crotch it is blowing a lot harder than we need. I decide that this is one of those times when we really should reef, but here the Devil comes in.

Over to the south and a little ahead, a modern thirty-plus-foot sloop is forging along in the same direction under mainsail alone. We are closing fast, and it is just too much fun to stop. The skipper of the sloop looks back, seems surprised to see us bearing down on him, and says something to his crew.

Lo, a foresail snaps out over his deck, and now he is as overcanvased as we are. *Penelope* is raging along now and continues to gain. I am straining all of my 225 pounds trying to hold her on course and am no longer sure that I can. Stampedes come to mind, runaway stagecoaches, and the Song of the Valkyries.

Slack tide now and the GPS says we are doing seven and a half knots over the bottom without any assist from the current. This is well over hull speed, and broad reaching at the very edge of control.

I'm wondering if something will break, or if excessive weather helm will force us into a broach, but mostly I am consumed by the sheer kinetic joy of this, the roaring sounds, and the lunging, surging, rushing, rhythmic motion. *Penelope* sweeps on past the other boat, and we don't look back.

The Valkyries continue their wild song as we pass Marshall Island to starboard, shoot up the middle of Jericho Bay, and blow into Burnt Coat Harbor like the Cannonball Express.

Pulpit Harbor to Burnt Coat in four and a half hours! A new record for sure. Approaching the mooring I am elated and spent at the same time. Great cruise! Great race! We are pretty good at this!

There's a little problem at the mooring, though. As we reach the spar buoy, we still have too much way on. The mooring trails too far astern as I cleat the pendant. I might have known that, sensing a certain growing hubris on my part, *Penelope* would want to reach into her bag of tricks and give me a little lesson.

Today *Penelope* will not round up docile and lady-like at her mooring, but jibe around wildly, a hoydenish, only half-trained thing. Members of the small audience that has gathered on shore will watch as the sail becomes entangled with the topping lift and a score of other things go wrong. They will note all this and carefully conceal smirks the next time we meet.

Playful, headstrong *Penelope* has done her little number and I am thoroughly humiliated. Gone is the euphoria of just moments ago.

As I furl her handsome tanbark sail, I can almost hear her quietly chuckling to herself.

21. Summer's Last Cruise

Lying in the darkness I am suddenly awakened as an icy drop of water crashes onto my forehead. Looking up through the open hatchway I can see a brilliant star-studded sky. There are no lights anywhere around this remote anchorage to compete with or diminish the splendor of the stars. You don't see skies like this much anymore, nor do your ears often experience this almost perfect silence, broken only by the distant murmur of small wavelets against shore.

I'm warm in my sleeping bag but the air is deliciously cold. The deck over my head is cold, too, and so is the curving shape of the hull by my right arm. This is why my breath has condensed on those surfaces, forming the droplets that have begun to fall here and there, and have woken me up. This is a sign that the seasons are changing. The nights are colder. Summer is ending. Such signs are everywhere.

For a week before this break in the weather there had been day after day of howling wind out of the northwest, another sign of the changing seasons. Sometimes NOAA promises that these autumnal nor'wester days will only be ten to fifteen knots, with possibly gusts to twenty, but we always take that with a grain of salt. The late-season nor'westers blow hard. We don't trust them for a minute, and we dislike them for other reasons, too. From home on Swan's Island, almost any desirable destination will be a hard beat.

Comes the break, and a dazzling warm day with wind from the south. NOAA speaks of a high that will last for a few days and we are off. Nothing ambitious, just a couple of days and nights while the going is good.

Off McGlathery Island at around 3 p.m. we think of stopping for the night, but the breeze is still fine, the sun is still warm, and we just don't want to stop. I spy the new wind turbines on distant Vinalhaven and think of heading that way, but the plan is not to get too far afield. *Penelope* is only minimally provisioned and I don't want to risk getting weathered in somewhere while supplies run out. What if we are stuck in some isolated spot and there is no more coffee and donuts? What if we run out of beer?

I decide that Pickering Cove, a quiet little gunkhole off Billings Cove toward the eastern side of Deer Isle, will make a fine destination, off the beaten track and well sheltered from the predicted southwest evening breeze. The passage there will be reaching and running through a cloud of small, jewel-like islands. And once arrived, we will still be within reasonable striking distance of home port.

Venturing into that maze of islands off Deer Isle is always an adventure because there are so many of them that it is frequently hard to tell which is which. You poke into narrow passageways not quite sure they are the right ones. It gets to be white-knuckle time as an already narrow passage gets narrower and everything starts to look wrong. There's supposed to be an opening around that point and a way between two more islands to open water, but where is it? And that ledge is way too far off that island . . . You press forward—not much choice really—and usually things open up revealing that you were right after all.

We point our nose in between what we believe to be Ram and Spruce Islands and hope for the best. There are ledges in every direction, but fortunately they all pretty much show when you need to see them. Coombs Island is now to port and Buckle Island, which juts out from Spruce, dead ahead. There are more ledges coming off Coombs and patches of brown and white, indicating shoal water seemingly everywhere.

We pass one ledge close enough to touch it with the boat hook. Behind Buckle is Devil Island and east of that is supposed to be the way out. But it doesn't open up for the longest time, and we start to wonder what really lies ahead. The tidal current is behind us, which is all well and good if we are where we think we are, but would be trouble if we had to turn around and try to tack our way out. Then suddenly the eastern end of Devil Island comes into view with open water beyond. Life is good.

There's a small, sandy beach on Devil and, perched above it here and there among the spruces, a modest collection of simple, old-fashioned gray-shingled cottages. It looks like those who summer here do so unencumbered by electricity, television, the Internet, and other of the double-edged "necessities" that make up the fabric of modern life.

I'm reminded of childhood sojourns on Monhegan Island where, due to a similar lack of services, life was more tribal. In the evenings people actually sat around fires and told stories. I learned a lot and I always thought it was a lot better than places where people went their separate ways to sit passively in front of electronic boxes.

Past Devil Island we leave a mass of ledges to port and head for Clam Island, a minimal sand-and-rock outcropping that stands out a brilliant white against the dark water. Then it is past the Shelldrake ledges, leaving Sheep Island to port. Wending our way through this island-, ledge-, and rock-studded seascape, we are careful to keep to water where the lobster buoys are thickest. If our chart-reading and landmark-picking skills fail us, as they sometimes do, the presence of lobster buoys is an almost unfailing indication that a given expanse of water has ample depth for a vessel of moderate draft.

An alternative way to pick one's way through such hazard-strewn waters, of course, would be to use a chart plotter, but that's cheating, and, just on general principles, you shouldn't become over-reliant on such methods. Save the GPS for times when the fog is swirling, the wind is howling, and you might lose your boat.

Rounding Eaton's Point at the western tip of Stinson's Neck now, I can see across to Pickering Cove and note that there are already a couple of boats in there. This would be fairly unusual at any time of year but is particularly so this late in the season. The wind, which is south, not the predicted southwest, is blowing directly in there, too, so I change plans and anchor in a nice lee under Stinson's Neck. It's a calm and beautiful evening, but I don't get to enjoy much of it because I'm soon out like a light.

Argos and *Penelope* in Billings Cove.

Morning dawns crisp and clear and I am awakened by another shot of icy water, more condensation from the deck over my head. There is a musical murmuring sound in the air, too. Looking out the hatch I see that we are surrounded by a huge raft of surf scoters. These oddly archaic-looking birds are cruising around, diving occasionally for mussels, and conversing quietly among themselves. Their sudden arrival from their summer haunts in the Arctic is the ultimate sign of the changing of the seasons.

There's a nice early-morning southwest breeze so I don't linger. Making sail and soon reaching along the Stinson's Neck shore, I head southeast for Swan's Island and home. Passing Lazygut Island, I admire a beautifully situated cottage on that small outcropping that I later learn belongs to my pen pal Clinton Trowbridge, author of *The Boat That Wouldn't Sink* and *The Crow Island Journal.* Anyone who loves these waters should be familiar with both of these.

The breeze is making up nicely, and by the time we are in the tide rip off the Hat Island ledges, *Penelope* is really flying. Hull speed and more.

To the west over Marshall Island massive clouds are forming in a sunshot cathedral-like effect. It is a morning of surpassing beauty and *Penelope* is charging along in fine fashion, doing her part to make it even better. It is a memorable, an awesome moment on the water. Tears come to my eyes because, for this year at least, it will be one of the last.

Afterword:
Living with an Elderly Marshall 22

When I bought my 1967 Marshall 22 in 1998, the survey revealed that the plywood cores in the rudder and transom had decayed and were in dangerous condition. Additionally there were areas of minor rash-like blistering at the turn of the bilge. I installed a new foam-cored rudder from Marshall Marine, and Hank Hinckley of what was then Great Harbor Marine in Bass Harbor built a new transom. Neither the yard, the surveyor, nor Bill Coleman, a fiberglass industry pioneer who summers in a fiberglass house here on Swan's Island, seemed to think the blistering (small pimples not visible from more than a couple of feet away) would become a problem, and, so far, they have been right.

The original gaff saddle became twisted and distorted over time, and failed to function properly. The replacement, which seems to be of more robust construction and design, has so far (four years) functioned flawlessly. The gaff collars are lined with plastic or Teflon where they come into contact with the mast, and this lining eventually wears out. Industrial carpeting glued to the collar with contact cement is suggested as a replacement. It was a year or two after this operation had been performed that the original mast collar failed.

The gaff collar is so essential to the functioning of the boat that I would buy a spare if they weren't so expensive (about four hundred dollars).

Otherwise, the boat has proved to be robust and trouble-free. Having heard that there have been occasional mast failures due to electrolytic corrosion where the aluminum mast is surrounded by a stainless-steel collar that supports the gooseneck among other things, I took a good look at the mast during one fall storage, and was surprised to find that it was partially full of water. Consequently I drilled a hole at the heel of the mast and always make sure the mast is inclined toward that drain when stored. There have been no problems with the seats, decks, bulkheads, or steering gear.

The first year I owned *Penelope* I did have a mystery leak that for a long time frustrated all attempts to find it. Temporary relief could be obtained by pouring sawdust into the centerboard trunk, where it was apparently drawn into the problem area and stopped the leak for a while, but the leak would always come back and it was bad enough so that I couldn't leave the boat untended for more than a day or two. Finally we found a crack in the bottom of the skeg, presumably separated from the interior of the boat by several feet of solid fiberglass. When this was filled with epoxy the problem was permanently solved.

When I first owned the boat, the port lights leaked and had to be rebedded. Additionally, the companionway hatch did not prove strong enough to take the weight of a 240-pound man on it and gave slightly so that from then on it scraped noisily on adjoining surfaces when being moved forward or back.

There is an area under the cabin sole, just aft of the head, that is sealed off from the rest of the boat (no limber hole in the transverse member at its aft end), which collects water from forward and the head area. I have to remove this water annually during fall storage with a turkey baster through a hole I have made in the cabin sole. Why not drill a limber hole? The hole would have to be made at a very awkward angle and uncomfortably close to the bottom. Could be done, but I have never cared to attempt it.

The forward hatch, which should be hinged, is not and is only dogged down with hooks and eyes similar to what you would find on a screen door. A friend of mine who also owns a Marshall 22 had his forward hatch cover mysteriously disappear during winter storage. It could have just as easily flown away and sunk in a nice reaching breeze.

I had to replace the centerboard pendant, which was worn, when I bought the boat, but otherwise have had no problems with the board. I understand that the pin upon which the board pivots can wear out and break, but checking it would involve a major repair that so far I have not felt was justified. The board itself, which I assume to have been made of the same composite construction as the defunct rudder and transom, has remained sound.

Like some Marshall 22s, *Penelope* is equipped with a bowsprit. While some purists claim a bowsprit has no place on a catboat, I think that view borders on the idiotic. As an aid to hauling anchors, particularly for single-handers, a bow roller on the sprit is invaluable. Standing on the tiny foredeck trying to haul your anchor while the boom is coming over and trying to push you overside is difficult and unnecessarily dangerous. With a bowsprit and roller you haul from the safety of the cockpit while maintaining a much better grip on overall control (steering, sheets, halyards, et cetera). The main anchor, my twenty-pound CQR, rides in the roller.

Just aft of the bowsprit at the very forward part of the house, I have added an opening bronze port light. Among the very few real flaws in the Marshall 22 are poor ventilation and light in the cabin. This, of course, is not a problem when the big companionway doors and hatch are open, but when the mosquitoes arrive and you have to button her up it sure becomes one. Aft of the port light is the aforementioned forehatch, and mounted in this is a solar vent I installed to help with ventilation. Just aft of this and to port is a dorade vent added for the same reason. I have yet to install a deck prism, but plan to when I am flush.

Farther aft on the cockpit combings just forward of the wheel are a pair of Wilcox Crittenden oarlock sockets. Oars are absolutely essential on an engineless boat like *Penelope* but I think even boats with motors should have them. Motors don't always work, and the wind doesn't always blow, but there are always currents that want to put you up on the rocks. The oars must be long enough to get a good bite in the water while clearing the side decks. I use a pair of

"Feathoars" long sculls that were designed for use with an Alden Ocean Shell. They work okay but would be even better if they were a foot or two longer. The oarlocks should be situated so that the backs of your legs can hold the wheel steady while you stand at the oars. Do not expect to enjoy rowing a Marshall 22.

Mounted on the rudder is a bronze step to help swimmers—voluntary or otherwise—get back on board. This piece of equipment is an option when you buy a boat from Marshall but it should be standard because its presence or the lack thereof can be a matter of life or death.

Also on the rudder and transom are a pair of gudgeons to take the pintles on the rudder stick, a piece of equipment that keeps the rudder from flopping around when the boat is at anchor or on a mooring. This also should be standard, but isn't. At best this flopping around causes wear in the steering system. At worst, in storms, it can cause costly damage.

I find the Marshall 22 with the original layout reasonably comfortable for a single-hander for periods of up to a couple of weeks, but my standards in this area are probably lower than those of most twenty-first-century Americans. There is no comfortable place to sit with back support belowdecks. The only place to be reasonably comfortable for extended periods is semi-reclining on the starboard bunk with your back up against the rear bulkhead. The marine supplier so aptly dubbed "Waste Marine" by the late Robb White sells a kind of truncated folding armchair that does serve well here. I place mine forward over the head and facing aft, where it works pretty well as a place below where you can comfortably relax and read.

Sitting on the starboard bunk with the centerboard-mounted folding table deployed is fine for mealtimes, but opening the table and getting your legs under it calls for major acrobatic contortions. Once you are so seated, you better be sure everything you want to eat and drink is close to hand, because getting up to fetch anything once again calls for major and complicated effort.

Cooking must be accomplished at some remove from the stove with the centerboard intervening. A very small person might be able to cook while sitting on or straddling the centerboard trunk.

The V-berths forward are, to my mind, suitable only for storage. They are short and, anyway, who wants to sleep with their head almost in the toilet? Along with the previously mentioned armchair, I keep large plastic bins of the kind Walmart stocks in such profusion up there and use them to store clothes, books, and food.

When cruising with my wife aboard, I find that everything you want access to is always under something else, and that logistics like making the bunk into a double—which more or less precludes any belowdecks activity other than lying down—are tedious to the point of unacceptability. The previous owner of my boat made fairly extensive cruises with his wife, two young daughters, and a dog. Of this I can only say, "Different strokes for different folks."

The cockpit is, of course, wonderfully comfortable, and this is where I manage to spend most of my time. A dodger over the companionway hatch would considerably improve conditions both above and below in rainy weather, but catboats with dodgers just don't look like catboats. Also very useful would be a permanent boom gallows.

One prized piece of equipment aboard is a "zero gravity" lounger, which is a lightweight folding chair that will assume any position from a cot-like horizontal to fully upright. It works well in the cockpit when at anchor or on a mooring and makes reading or dozing as comfortable as they could ever be at home—or more so. Before I had the antigravity chair, I used to bring up the big bunk cushion from below and lay it crosswise over the seats and across the cockpit deck. With your legs up on one seat and your back against the other, this was a pretty comfortable way to loll away a windless afternoon.

It is in the area of performance that the Marshall 22 comes into her own, and here, along with the way she looks, is why we love her. She is weatherly, fast, nimble, and dry. Simple to handle, no jib sheets to hassle with, and no deck-sweeping genoa to peer around.

You can see where you are going, and you are going there efficiently and fast. On a few occasions I have seen the GPS register seven and a half knots over the ground with no help from the current, and cruising at six knots is not at all unusual. She keeps up with or passes cruising boats of up to or sometimes more than thirty feet. And this on all points of sail. The idea that catboats, at least engineless ones, don't go well to windward is just not true. She is also quick and reliable in stays. In fact, in the seventeen years I have owned her she has never missed stays even once.

Even in the frequently boisterous open ocean waters around Swan's Island this twenty-two-footer is amazingly dry and capable. Spray almost never reaches the cockpit no matter what you are thrashing into. I don't think I have ever felt it necessary to wear foul-weather gear when it was not raining.

Penelope was fast and weatherly before I took the engine out, and afterward she was more so. The general quality of her gear and working parts is very high, though the interior appointments of some of the earlier boats, including mine, are a little rough. This situation has changed for the better over time. Comparing my boat with later examples of the Marshall 22 I have examined, I would say that mine is a boat, and those later examples are yachts.

I feel confident that in her current state she will last longer than I will, and I can't think of many craft of any size or price that I would trade her for. I've owned several cruising boats and *Penelope* has been just more flat-out fun than any of the others.

Penelope in our back yard.
Note the absence of a propeller or propeller aperture.

W. R. Cheney has worked as the sheriff in the Gaslight Club in Paris and sold Volkswagens in Afghanistan. For more than forty years he was a professional photographer and photojournalist in Europe and the United States. During much of that period he managed to own boats and spend an inordinate amount of time using them, most notably in the Bahamas, along the US eastern seaboard, and on the Baie d'Arcachon. He, his wife Kendra, and their English setter Sparky currently divide their time between Swan's Island, Maine, where he sails the engineless Marshall 22 *Penelope*, and Lady's Island, South Carolina, where he cruises and races the Marshall Sanderling *Shorebird*. Cheney and *Shorebird* are two-time winners of the Savannah, Georgia, to Beaufort, South Carolina, Classic Boat Rally.